# ACKNOWLEDGEMENTS

With thanks to all the good friends who delved into their recipe collections, particularly Marie Toshack and her family of country cooks, also Ros Bowden, Joan Edison, Jean Higgins, Keith McLean, John Sears, and Renate Yates.

First published in Great Britain 1992 by Aurum Press Ltd,
10 Museum Street, London WC1A 1JS
Copyright © Collins Angus & Robertson Publishers Pty Limited 1991

A catalogue record for this book is available from the British Library.

ISBN 1 85410 214 1

10 9 8 7 6 5 4 3 2 1
1996 1995 1994 1993 1992

First published in Australia by Collins Angus & Robertson Publishers Pty Limited

Cover photography by Scott Cameron

Printed in Australia by Griffin Press Ltd

# CONTENTS

# $\mathcal{I}$NTRODUCTION

M aking jams, jellies and marmalades is like bottling sunshine: a way of storing memories. Peach trees sagging with abundance, a patch of strawberries—even a cumquat (kumquat) tree covered with golden fruit in a pot on your balcony or in the conservatory.

There is something magical about home preserving. Before your eyes a mixture of fruit juice and sugar becomes a jelly that drops like jewels from a spoon.

The tradition goes back a long way. In the 16th century a mixture of fruit pulp and sugar was cooked until solid (something like today's fruit pastes) and eaten as a sweetmeat. In the 18th century this evolved into a mixture of fruit and sugar syrup, more like jam as we know it. By late last century, jam was being manufactured commercially on a large scale and became one of the staple foods of the poor.

Spreading it on toast is only one of its uses. Consider jam as a luscious filling for cakes and tarts. You can also use jellies this way, but their main use is as a delicious accompaniment to meat, poultry and game. Marmalade, as we know it, originated in Scotland in the 18th century and it has been incorporated into many traditional Scottish recipes for sauces, puddings and cakes. Try serving it with ham or duck like a chutney or relish.

This book also includes some recipes for fruit liqueurs. They are fun to make and a great way to finish a special dinner.

Making jams, jellies and marmalades is a tradition that shouldn't be allowed to die out. It may seem simpler to take a jar from the supermarket shelf, but you can't buy the same satisfaction. Or the same variety. Convenience foods certainly have their place, but why not use the extra time they give you to indulge in some more leisurely culinary pursuits?

Making jams, jellies and marmalades is one of the simplest and most satisfying ways of preserving the bounty of summer. By following simple techniques you can make jam, jelly, or marmalade from almost any type of fruit and some vegetables. But it's important to bear in mind that the finished product will be only as good as the ingredients used.

Fruit should be as freshly picked as possible and in most cases slightly under-ripe. Jams, jellies and marmalades made from over-ripe fruit will not set or keep as well. If the fruit is home-grown, gather it in the morning after the dew has dried. Fruit picked when wet deteriorates quickly. Do not wipe off the bloom (on peaches, plums etc) until ready to use; the bloom helps keep fruit fresh. Wash fruit thoroughly just before using—it's important to remove dust and the residue of any insecticides.

Most of the following recipes are for small quantities as the long cooking time required for large quantities can result in loss of flavour. Jams that are cooked quickly retain more of the original fruit flavour. If you have a large quantity of home-grown produce use it in different preserves rather than making just one type.

# PECTIN

For successful jam, jelly and marmalade making, it's essential to have a balance of acid and pectin. Pectin is a natural setting agent present in some but not all fruit. As fruit ripens pectin diminishes, which is why it's best to use fruit that is just ripe or slightly under-ripe. Some fruits are naturally low in pectin but they can be combined with high pectin fruits, for instance blackberry with apple, to give a good result. If fruit is low in acid extra can be added, usually in the form of lemon juice. Lemon juice also contains pectin, so adding it boosts both acid and pectin.

High pectin fruits include: cooking apples, crab apples, lemons, limes, oranges (particularly sour varieties such as Seville), grapefruit, quinces, plums, currants, gooseberries and cranberries.

Medium pectin fruits include: apricots, loganberries, raspberries, sweet apples and guavas.

Low pectin fruits include: pears, peaches, cherries, figs, pineapples, strawberries, blackberries (bramble) and melons.

*Testing for pectin:* Cook a little of the fruit until the juice runs out. Put 1 teaspoon of the cooled juice into a bowl and add 3 teaspoons of methylated spirits (rubbing alcohol). Stir the mixture and leave it for a minute. If a large, jelly-like clot forms, the fruit is high in pectin, if a few smaller clots form the fruit is medium in pectin and if it breaks into a mass of small pieces the fruit is low in pectin.

*Commercial pectin:* You can buy powdered pectin at health food stores, some delicatessens and specialty outlets. Simply follow the manufacturer's instructions. It gives a reliable set, but the flavour of the jam or jelly is never as good as one that has set naturally.

# SUGAR

The other important ingredient in jams, jellies and marmalades is sugar. It is the preservative—jams with too little sugar may have a good natural fruit flavour, but they will not keep well. Sugar also affects setting, so it's important to get the proportion right. The amount of sugar is determined by the pectin content of the fruit and should represent approximately 60 per cent of the final weight of the jam, jelly, or marmalade. You can get a good idea of the final yield of a recipe by looking at the amount of sugar used. A high pectin fruit will require more sugar than a low pectin fruit. The reason is that jam made with a high pectin fruit reaches setting point faster than one made with a low pectin fruit. There is less evaporation of liquid and consequently a higher yield. Here is a guide to the amount of sugar needed for the different types of fruit.

*High pectin fruit:* 2½ cups (20 oz) sugar to 2 cups (1 lb) fruit.

*Medium pectin fruit:* 2 cups (1 lb) sugar to 2 cups (1 lb) fruit.

*Low pectin fruit:* 1½ cups (12 oz) sugar to 2 cups (1 lb) fruit.

Sugar is added after the fruit has cooked—with a few exceptions, for instance some berry jams. Once the sugar has been added, the fruit will not get any softer—in fact, it may toughen if cooking is prolonged. Sugar measurements in this book are for ordinary white granular sugar, although preserving or lump sugar can also be used, with the advantage of less scum and a clearer appearance. Greasing the preserving pan with butter or adding a small knob of butter at the end of cooking also reduces scum and produces a lovely clear jam.

Sugar should be dissolved as quickly as possible to prevent loss of flavour in the final product. You can speed up the dissolving process by warming sugar in the oven before adding it to the jam—simply spread sugar in a shallow baking dish and warm in a slow oven for about 10 minutes. Make sure the sugar is thoroughly dissolved before being brought to boiling point or the jam may crystallise. Do not stir jam after it reaches boiling point, although you can use a spoon to check that it is not sticking to the bottom of the pan.

Honey is not a substitute for sugar in jams, jellies and marmalades, but you can use it for a lovely change of flavour. You can replace up to half the amount of sugar in a recipe with honey, but your jam or jelly will not keep as well, and it will require longer cooking. The set will also be much softer. Honey can also be added purely as a flavouring: ½ cup (4 oz) honey to 6 cups (3 lb) sugar.

## TEST FOR SETTING POINT

After about 10 minutes of rapid boiling—this means a rolling boil, which cannot be stirred down with a spoon—it's time to test for setting. Move the preserving pan off the heat and drop a teaspoon of the mixture onto a saucer that has been chilled in the fridge. Return the saucer to the fridge (or freezer) to cool. In the case of jam the surface should be set and wrinkle when pushed with a finger. It should be a spreadable consistency. Jellies and marmalades should be a firm mass. If jam is not set, return the pan to the heat and test again after about five minutes.

You can also use a sugar (candy) thermometer to test for set. Stand the thermometer in hot water before immersing it in the jam—make sure it doesn't touch the bottom or it may break. Setting point is approximately 105°C (220°F).

Once setting point has been reached, the jam should be skimmed with a slotted spoon to remove any scum that may have formed on the surface. Do this only at the end of cooking—it's wasteful to do it more than once. Don't forget that greasing the preserving pan with a little butter or adding a small knob of butter at the end of cooking will reduce the need for skimming.

# BOTTLING

M ost jams and jellies are poured into warm jars as soon as cooking finishes. Marmalades and jams with whole fruit or large pieces of fruit should be left to stand for 5 to 10 minutes until a thin skin forms on top, before stirring gently and pouring into warm jars. This prevents fruit from rising to the top.

*To prepare jars:* wash thoroughly in hot water, then transfer to a cold oven. Turn oven to the lowest temperature and leave for about 20 minutes until the jars are warm and dry. It's important to pour the hot jam into warm jars—if cold they may crack. You can also reduce the risk of cracking or breaking by standing a metal spoon or fork in the jar before pouring in the jam.

It's a good idea to spread a few layers of newspaper or a tea towel underneath the jars before filling. Never stand jars on a cold surface, such as a marble slab, to fill.

Opinion differs as to whether jam should be sealed when hot or cold. The experts agree, however, that it shouldn't be sealed when warm, as this can cause mould. If using metal or plastic screw-on lids, seal when hot. If using paper jam covers, lay the waxed surface on the jam when hot, then add the transparent cover when the jam is cold and secure with a rubber band or string.

Paraffin wax makes an excellent seal for jams. You can buy it at pharmacies and supermarkets (US). Melt it in the top of a double saucepan (boiler) (or an old enamel or aluminium teapot or kettle) over a very low heat—do not heat more than necessary to melt. Pour over hot jam or jelly and leave to cool. If necessary, put on a second layer of wax. Seal with a screw-top lid or paper, then cover when cold.

Always label jars with the date and type of preserve. Store in a cool dark place—storing in a light warm place can cause deterioration of colour and fermentation. Do not store near the stove as steam can cause mould on the jam.

# EQUIPMENT

*Preserving pan:* this should be large and wide to allow for the evaporation that is an essential part of the jam making process. It should be made of aluminium, stainless steel, or enamel. If using an aluminium pan, do not leave the fruit to stand in it for much more than an hour. You can use an ordinary saucepan, provided it is big enough. The preserving pan should never be more than two-thirds full at any stage— during rapid boiling it can easily overflow, with disastrous consequences.

*Jars:* save jars with screw-top lids for jam, jelly and marmalade making. You can buy special paper covers for jam, but I find these somewhat unsatisfactory once the jars have been opened. If recycling jars, clean off old labels by soaking in hot water, then washing. If any label or sticking solution remains, you can clean it off easily with a little methylated spirits. You can buy jam labels at most stationery shops. It's important to label each new batch with the date and type.

*Other utensils:* muslin (cheesecloth) bags, scales, measuring jug, sieve, wooden spoon, slotted metal spoon for skimming, a ladle and a heatproof jug for transferring jam from the preserving pan to jars.

*Making jams, jellies and marmalades in a pressure cooker (canner):* The first step, breaking down the fruit, is accomplished much faster in a pressure cooker. And the natural colour and flavour is retained to a great degree. Once you add the sugar, use the pressure cooker like an ordinary saucepan—its thick bottom will help prevent burning and sticking during the reduction/evaporation process. Never fill a pressure cooker more than half-full for jam, jelly, or marmalade making.

# JAMS

## Apple and Almond Jam

This jam is good in a steamed pudding.

| | |
|---|---|
| 1 kg (2 lb) cooking apples | 4 cups (2 lb) sugar |
| 2 cups (16 fl oz) water | 4 tablespoons blanched, slivered almonds |
| Thinly peeled rind and juice of 1 lemon | |

Peel, core and chop the apples, reserving the peel and cores. Put the apples and water into a preserving pan. Put the lemon rind into a muslin (cheesecloth) bag with the apple peel and cores, and add to the pan with the lemon juice. Bring to the boil and simmer until the apple is pulpy. Remove the bag, squeezing the juice into the pan. Add the sugar and stir until dissolved. Add the almonds and stir in, then boil rapidly until setting point is reached. Skim and pour into jars. Seal.

*Makes about 7 cups (3½ lb)*

---

◆

---

*Apples are one of the most ancient of fruits*
*— they were cultivated by the ancient*
*Egyptians in the 12th century BC.*

### Apple and Pear Jam

500 g (1 lb) cooking
   apples
500 g (1 lb) pears
2 cups (16 fl oz)
   water

1 lemon
6 cloves
4 cups (2 lb) sugar

Peel, core and chop the apples and pears, reserving the peel and cores. Put the apples, pears and water into a preserving pan. Thinly peel the rind from the lemon and put this in a muslin (cheesecloth) bag with the cloves, peelings and cores. Add the bag to the pan. Squeeze the lemon and add the juice to the pan. Bring to the boil and simmer until the fruit is tender and pulpy. Remove the bag, squeezing out the juice. Add the sugar and stir over a gentle heat, until dissolved, then boil rapidly until setting point is reached. Skim. Pour into jars and seal.

*Makes about 7 cups (3½ lb)*

## Apple Ginger Jam

| | |
|---|---|
| 1 kg (2 lb) cooking apples | 2 cups (16 fl oz) water |
| 6-8 teaspoons finely chopped (minced) fresh ginger (ginger root) | Grated rind and juice of 1 lemon |
| | 4 cups (2 lb) sugar |

Peel, core and chop the apples, reserving the peel and cores. Put the apples, ginger and water into a preserving pan. Put the apple peel and cores in a muslin (cheesecloth) bag and add it to the pan. Add the lemon rind and juice to the pan. Bring to the boil and simmer until the apples are tender and pulpy. Remove the bag, squeezing out the juice. Add the sugar, stirring until dissolved. Boil rapidly until setting point is reached. Skim. Pour into jars. Seal.

*Makes about 7 cups (3½ lb)*

## Apricot Jam

| | |
|---|---|
| 1 kg (2 lb) apricots, firm but ripe | Juice of 1 lemon |
| 1 cup (8 fl oz) water | 4 cups (2 lb) sugar |

Cut the apricots in half and remove the stones (pits). Crack about half the stones and remove the kernels, the edible seed. Blanch the kernels by plunging into boiling water for about 1 minute, then remove the skins and split each kernel in half. Set the kernels aside.

Put the apricots into a preserving pan with the water and lemon juice. Bring to the boil and simmer until the fruit is soft, then stir in the sugar until dissolved. Boil rapidly. About 10 minutes before setting point is reached, add the kernels. When setting point is reached, skim and pour into jars. Seal.

*Makes about 7 cups (3½ lb)*

### Pressure Cooker (Canner) Dried Apricot Jam

| | |
|---|---|
| 500 g (1 lb) dried apricot halves | Grated rind and juice of 1 lemon |
| 5 cups (40 fl oz) boiling water | 4 cups (2 lb) sugar |
| | 50 g (2 oz) blanched almonds, chopped |

Roughly chop the apricots and put them into the pressure cooker. Pour in the boiling water. Leave the apricots to soften, then add the lemon rind and juice, put the lid on and pressure cook for 10 minutes. Remove from heat and when the pressure reduces, remove the lid and add the sugar. Return to heat, uncovered, and stir to dissolve the sugar. Add the almonds, and cook rapidly until setting point is reached—test after 5 minutes. Skim. Leave for 5 minutes before stirring gently and pouring into jars. Seal.

*Makes about 7 cups (3½ lb)*

### Apricot and Passionfruit (Purple Granadilla) Jam

| | |
|---|---|
| 1 kg (2 lb) apricots | Pulp of 6 passionfruit |
| 1 cup (8 fl oz) water | (purple granadilla) |
| Juice of 1 lemon | 4 cups (2 lb) sugar |

Halve the apricots and remove the stones (pits). Put the apricots into a preserving pan with the water and lemon juice. Bring to the boil and simmer until the fruit is soft. Add the passionfruit, then stir in the sugar until dissolved. Boil rapidly until setting point is reached. Skim. Pour into jars and seal.

*Makes about 7 cups (3½ lb)*

### Banana Jam

It may sound unlikely, but this makes a delicious filling for cakes—and children love it spread on bread. It won't reach setting point like an ordinary jam, but is ready when it achieves a good spreading consistency.

| | |
|---|---|
| *3 lemons* | *8 ripe bananas* |
| *3 cups (1½ lb) sugar* | *2.5 cm (1 inch) piece* |
| *3 cups (24 fl oz)* | *fresh ginger (ginger* |
| *water* | *root), peeled* |

Thinly peel the rind from the lemons and slice into thin slivers, then squeeze the juice. Bring the sugar and water to the boil in a preserving pan, and simmer for 10 minutes. Mash the bananas and add to the preserving pan with the lemon juice and rind, and the ginger. Cook this slowly for about 40 minutes, stirring frequently. Remove the ginger and pour into jars. Seal. Store in the refrigerator—will not keep for more than a few weeks.

*Makes about 5 cups (2½ lb)*

### Blackberry (Bramble) Jam

| | |
|---|---|
| *1 kg (2 lb) black-* | *Juice of 2 lemons* |
| *berries (brambles)* | *1 kg (2 lb) sugar* |
| *44 ml (1½ fl oz) water* | |

Pick through the blackberries, then put them into a preserving pan with the water and lemon juice. Simmer until the fruit is tender. Add the sugar, stirring until dissolved. Boil rapidly until setting point is reached. Skim. Pour into jars and seal.

*Makes about 7 cups (3½ lb)*

### Blackberry (Bramble) and Apple Jam

*1 kg (2 lb) black-*
*berries (brambles)*
*¾ cup (6 fl oz) water*

*3 cooking apples, peeled,*
*cored and sliced*
*4 cups (2 lb) sugar*

Pick through the blackberries, then put them into a preserving pan with half the water. Simmer until tender. Put the apples into a saucepan with the remaining water and simmer until pulpy. Add the apple pulp to the blackberries. Add the sugar, stirring until dissolved. Boil rapidly until setting point is reached. Skim. Pour into jars and seal.

*Makes about 7 cups (3½ lb)*

## Cherry Jam

1½ kg (3½ lb) cherries  
Juice of 1 lemon

Water  
3 cups (1½ lb) sugar

Remove the stones (pits) from the cherries and tie them in a muslin (cheesecloth) bag. Put the cherries, stones and lemon juice into a preserving pan with just enough water to cover the bottom of the pan. Bring slowly to the boil and simmer until the cherries are tender. Remove the muslin bag. Add the sugar, stirring until dissolved, then boil rapidly until setting point is reached. Skim. Pour into jars and seal.

*Makes about 5 cups (2½ lb)*

## Spiced Cherry Jam

Allow this spicy preserve to mature for 6 weeks before using—it makes a lovely filling for tarts.

4 cups (2 lb) sugar  
1 cup (8 fl oz) white  
   vinegar  
1 teaspoon ground  
   cinnamon

¼ teaspoon ground  
   cloves  
1 kg (2 lb) pitted  
   cherries

Put the sugar and vinegar into a preserving pan with spices. Bring to the boil, stirring to dissolve the sugar. Add the cherries and simmer until the jam is thick. Pour into jars and seal.

*Makes about 7 cups (3½ lb)*

NOTE: *For both cherry jam recipes Morello cherries are best, but other kinds of cherries may be substituted.*

### Cumquat (Kumquat) Conserve

This preserve is good with ice-cream.

| | |
|---|---|
| 1 kg (2 lb) cumquats | Salt |
| (kumquats) | 4 cups (2 lb) sugar |
| Water | |

Put the whole cumquats into a preserving pan with just enough water to cover, and a handful of salt. Bring to the boil and simmer until the cumquats are tender. Drain off and discard the salted water, then transfer the cumquats to a bowl. Add enough fresh water to cover the cumquats and stand for about 1 hour, then make a syrup with the sugar and 4 cups (32 fl oz) of the water from the cumquats.

When the syrup comes to the boil, add the drained cumquats and boil rapidly until setting point is reached. Skim. Stand for 10 minutes, then stir gently and pour into jars. Seal.

*Makes about 7 cups (3½ lb)*


### Date and Apple Jam

| | |
|---|---|
| 1 kg (2 lb) cooking | Juice of 2 limes |
| apples, peeled | Juice of 1 orange |
| and cored | 1½ cups (12 oz) dates, |
| 4 cups (2 lb) sugar | pitted and chopped |

Put the apples, sugar and juice into a preserving pan and bring slowly to the boil, stirring to dissolve the sugar. Add the dates and boil rapidly for about 20 minutes. Pour into jars and seal.

*Makes about 7 cups (3½ lb)*

## Fig Jam (1)

| | |
|---|---|
| *1 kg (2 lb) fresh figs* | *2 lemons* |
| *½ cup (4 fl oz) water* | *3 cups (1½ lb) sugar* |

Remove the stalks from the figs and slice. Put into a preserving pan with the water. Squeeze the juice from the lemons, then tie the rind and pith in a muslin (cheesecloth) bag and add to the preserving pan with the juice. Bring to the boil and simmer until the figs are soft. Remove the muslin bag. Add the sugar, stirring until dissolved. Boil rapidly for 20 minutes or until setting point is reached. Skim. Pour into jars. Seal.

*Makes about 5 cups (2½ lb)*

## Fig Jam (2)

The addition of vinegar in this version adds a touch of sharpness that cuts the heavy sweetness of the figs.

| | |
|---|---|
| *1 kg (2 lb) fresh figs* | *1 cup (8 fl oz)* |
| *4 cups (2 lb) sugar* | *vinegar* |
| *1 cup (8 fl oz) water* | |

Remove the stalks from the figs and chop. Bring the sugar, water and vinegar to the boil, stirring until the sugar has dissolved. Boil rapidly for 5 minutes, then add the figs, and simmer until setting point is reached. Pour into jars and seal.

*Makes about 7 cups (3½ lb)*

### Dried Fig and Walnut Jam

This is good spread on bread with cheese.

*1 kg (2 lb) dried figs*　　　*6 cups (3 lb) sugar*
*3¾ cups (30 fl oz)*　　　*4 tablespoons finely*
　　*water*　　　　　　　*chopped (minced)*
*Juice of 1 lemon*　　　　*walnuts*

Soak the figs in water overnight. Drain and rinse in fresh water. Remove the stems, chop roughly and put into a preserving pan with the water and lemon juice. Bring to the boil and simmer gently until the figs are soft. Add the sugar, stirring until dissolved, then boil rapidly until the mixture thickens. Stir in the walnuts, then pour into jars. Seal.

*Makes about 10 cups (5 lb)*

## Brandied Fruit Jam

225 g (8 oz) red-
   currants
225 g (8 oz)
   raspberries
225 g (8 oz) cherries,
   pitted

225 g (8 oz)
   gooseberries, topped
   and tailed
2½ cups (20 fl oz)
   water
4 cups (2 lb) sugar
60 ml (2 fl oz) brandy

Put the fruit into a preserving pan with the water. Bring to the boil and simmer until the fruit is soft. Add the sugar, stirring until dissolved. Stir in the brandy, then boil rapidly until setting point is reached. Skim. Pour into jars and seal.

*Makes about 10 cups (5 lb)*

NOTE: *Morello cherries are best for this recipe but other kinds of cherries may be substituted.*

## Fruit Salad Jam

500 g (1 lb) peaches
500 g (1 lb) apricots
500 g (1 lb) pineapple,
   peeled, cored and
   shredded

Pulp of 4 passionfruit
   (purple granadilla)
2 bananas
6 cups (3 lb) sugar

Slice the peaches and apricots, removing the stones (pits). Put into a preserving pan with the pineapple and passionfruit pulp. Bring slowly to the boil and simmer until the fruit is soft—if necessary add a little water, but the fruit should cook in its juice. Slice the bananas and add to the pan, then add the sugar, stirring until dissolved. Boil rapidly until setting point is reached. Skim. Pour into jars and seal.

*Makes about 10 cups (5 lb)*

## Grape Jam

1 kg (2 lb) seedless
    grapes
Juice of 1 lemon
½ cup (4 fl oz) water
4 cups (2 lb) sugar

Put the grapes into a preserving pan and mash with a potato masher. Add the lemon juice and water, bring slowly to the boil and simmer, stirring frequently for 10 minutes or until the grapes are pulpy. Add the sugar, stirring until dissolved, then boil rapidly until setting point is reached. Skim. Pour into jars and seal.

*Makes about 7 cups (3½ lb)*

## Grape and Orange Jam

1 kg (2 lb) seedless
    grapes
Juice and grated rind
    of 2 oranges
½ cup (4 fl oz) water
4 cups (2 lb) sugar
1 teaspoon citric acid

Put the grapes into a preserving pan and mash with a potato masher. Add the orange juice, rind and water, then bring slowly to the boil and simmer, stirring frequently, for 10 minutes or until the grapes are pulpy. Add the sugar and citric acid, stirring until dissolved, then boil rapidly until setting point is reached. Skim. Pour into jars and seal.

*Makes about 7 cups (3½ lb)*

◆

*Egyptian hieroglyphics dating back to 2400 BC describe grape and wine production.*

## Lemon and Carrot Jam

| | |
|---|---|
| 2 large lemons | 2 medium-sized |
| 5 cups (40 fl oz) | carrots |
| water | 4 cups (2 lb) sugar |

Slice the lemons thinly and put into a bowl. Bring the water to a boil and pour it over the lemons. Grate (shred) the carrots, add to the lemons and let it stand for 1 hour. Put the lemons, carrots and water into a preserving pan, bring to the boil and simmer until the lemon rind is tender—about 1 hour. Add the sugar, stirring to dissolve, then boil rapidly until setting point is reached. Skim. Leave for 10 minutes before pouring into jars. Seal when cool.

*Makes about 7 cups (3½ lb)*

## Melon and Pineapple Jam

| | |
|---|---|
| 1 kg (2 lb) honeydew | ½ teaspoon salt |
| melon, diced | Juice of 2 lemons |
| 1 kg (2 lb) pineapple, | 8 cups (4 lb) sugar |
| peeled, cored and | |
| shredded | |

Put the diced honeydew melon and shredded pineapple into a preserving pan with the salt, lemon juice and 1 cup (8 oz) of the sugar. Cover and cook gently for about 45 minutes, stirring occasionally. Add a little water if it starts to stick. Add the remaining sugar and cook, uncovered, for another 30 minutes, stirring frequently. Pour into jars and seal.

*Makes about 14 cups (7 lb)*

## Mulberry Jam

If you are lucky enough to have a mulberry tree don't leave the fruit to the birds. This jam makes a lovely filling for tarts served with cream.

2 kg (4 lb) mulberries          6 cups (3 lb) sugar
1 teaspoon citric or
     tartaric acid

Remove stalks from the mulberries and put into a preserving pan over low heat. Simmer gently for 15 minutes, then add the citric or tartaric acid and warmed sugar (see p. 4), stirring until dissolved. Cook rapidly, stirring occasionally, until setting point is reached. Skim. Allow to stand for 5 minutes before stirring gently and pouring into jars. Seal.

*Makes about 10 cups (5 lb)*

## Passionfruit (Purple Granadilla) Jam

28 passionfruit                    Juice of 1 lemon
     (purple granadilla)       5 cups (2½ lb) sugar
1 cup (8 fl oz) water

Cut the passionfruit in half and scoop out the pulp and seeds. Take a quarter of the passionfruit skins and put them into a saucepan with enough water to cover, and boil for 30 minutes or until quite tender. Drain, then scrape as much pulp as possible from the skins. Add this to the reserved pulp and seeds.

Pour the pulp into a preserving pan and add the water, lemon juice and sugar. Bring to the boil, stirring gently to dissolve the sugar, then boil rapidly until setting point is reached. Leave for 10 minutes before pouring into jars. Seal when cool.

*Makes about 8½ cups (4¼ lb)*

## Pawpaw (Papaya) Jam

| | |
|---|---|
| 1 large pawpaw (papaya), finely diced | Juice of 2 limes |
| 1 tablespoon finely chopped (minced) fresh ginger (ginger root) | Sugar—an amount equal to the diced pawpaw |

Put all ingredients into a bowl and leave overnight. Transfer to a preserving pan and cook gently, stirring to dissolve the sugar. Simmer for about 20 minutes, then pour into jars and seal. Store in refrigerator.

*Makes about 7 cups (3½ lb)*


## Peach Jam

| | |
|---|---|
| 1 cooking apple, chopped, peel, core and seeds included | 1½ cups (12 fl oz) water |
| Rind of 2 lemons | 1 teaspoon ground allspice (Jamaica pepper) |
| 2 kg (4 lb) peaches | 6 cups (3 lb) sugar |

Tie the apple and lemon rind in a muslin (cheesecloth) bag and put into a preserving pan. Slice the peaches and remove the stones (pits). Add the sliced peaches and water to the preserving pan. Bring slowly to the boil and simmer for 15 minutes or until the peaches are soft. Remove the muslin bag, squeezing the juice into the pan. Add the allspice and sugar, stirring to dissolve the sugar, then boil rapidly until setting point is reached. Skim. Allow to stand for 10 minutes before pouring into jars. Seal.

*Makes about 10 cups (5 lb)*

## Peach and Passionfruit
## (Purple Granadilla) Jam

Peaches and passionfruit make a lovely aromatic combination.

*1 kg (2 lb) peaches*
*3 cups (1½ lb) sugar*
*Juice of 2 lemons*

*Pulp of 4 passion-*
*fruit (purple*
*granadilla)*

Skin the peaches (plunge into boiling water if the skins do not slip off easily) and slice, removing the stones (pits). Put into a bowl and sprinkle with half the sugar, and leave to stand for 1 hour. Put into a preserving pan and bring to the boil, then simmer until the fruit is tender. Add the rest of the sugar, then the lemon juice and cook rapidly until setting point is reached. Mix in the passionfruit pulp and cook for a few minutes longer. Skim. Leave for 5 minutes before pouring into jars. Seal.

*Makes about 5 cups (2½ lb)*

### Pear Jam

2 kg (4 lb) pears
2 cups (16 fl oz) water
Juice and rind of 3
    lemons

4 cloves
5 cups (2½ lb) sugar

Peel and core the pears, then chop and put into a preserving pan with the water and lemon juice. Tie the lemon rind and cloves in a muslin (cheesecloth) bag, and add it to the pan. Bring slowly to the boil and simmer until the fruit is soft. Remove the muslin bag, squeezing the juice into the pan. Add the sugar, stirring until dissolved, then boil rapidly until setting point is reached. Skim. Pour into jars. Seal.

*Makes about 8½ cups (4¼ lb)*

## Pear and Ginger Jam

| | |
|---|---|
| 2 kg (4 lb) pears | 3–4 teaspoons finely |
| 2 cups (16 fl oz) water | chopped (minced) |
| Juice and rind of 3 | preserved ginger |
| lemons | 5 cups (2½ lb) sugar |

Peel and core the pears, then chop and put into a preserving pan with the water and lemon juice. Tie the lemon rind in a muslin (cheesecloth) bag and add to the pan. Bring slowly to the boil and simmer until the fruit is soft. Remove the muslin bag, squeezing any juice into the pan. Add the ginger and sugar, stirring until dissolved, then boil rapidly until setting point is reached. Skim. Pour into jars. Seal.

*Makes about 8½ cups (4¼ lb)*

## Persimmon Jam

Persimmons are a native of America. The early settlers used them to make puddings and a type of beer, as well as jams and jellies. At a dinner for the Grand Duke Alexis of Russia held in 1872 during his visit to Topeka, Kansas, one of the dishes on the menu was roast possum with persimmon jelly. This exotic preserve is certainly more suited to the dinner table than breakfast. Use it as a filling for tarts or serve it with cream or ice-cream.

| | |
|---|---|
| 1½ kg (3 lb) | 1 cup (8 fl oz) orange |
| persimmons | juice |
| 2 cups (1 lb) sugar | Grated rind of 1 lemon |

Make a cross cut on the pointed end of each persimmon and peel the skin back to the stem. Remove the seeds and puree the flesh in a food processor. Put the persimmon pulp into a saucepan with the other ingredients. Cook over a low heat, stirring constantly, until thick and opaque—about 15 minutes. Do not boil. Pour into jars and seal. Store in the refrigerator.

*Makes about 3½ cups (1¾ lb)*

## Pineapple Jam

| | |
|---|---|
| *2 kg (4 lb) pineapple* | *2 lemons* |
| *2½ cups (20 fl oz) water* | *8 cups (4 lb) sugar* |

Chop the pineapple into small pieces and put into a preserving pan with the water. Squeeze the juice from the lemons, then tie the squeezed lemons in a muslin (cheesecloth) bag. Add the juice and bag to the preserving pan. Bring to the boil and simmer until the pineapple is soft. Remove the muslin bag. Put the pineapple into a bowl and leave to cool, then stir in the sugar and leave overnight.

Return ingredients to the pan and bring to the boil, stirring to dissolve the sugar. Boil rapidly until setting point is reached. Skim. Pour the jam into jars and seal.

*Makes about 14 cups (7 lb)*

## Pineapple and Apple Jam

Pineapple is low in pectin so apples are added to give a better set without overwhelming the flavour of the pineapple.

| | |
|---|---|
| *1 kg (2 lb) pineapple* | *2½ cups (20 fl oz)* |
| *(slightly under-ripe),* | *water* |
| *peeled, cored and* | *Juice of 1 lemon* |
| *shredded* | *6 cups (3 lb) sugar* |
| *1 kg (2 lb) cooking* | |
| *apples* | |

Put the pineapple into a preserving pan. Peel and chop the apples and add to the pan. Tie the apple peel, cores and seeds in a muslin (cheesecloth) bag and add to the pan. Pour in the water and lemon juice then simmer, stirring frequently, until the fruit is soft. Add the warmed sugar (see p. 4) and bring slowly to the boil, stirring until the sugar has dissolved. Boil rapidly until setting point is reached. Skim. Allow to stand for 5 minutes before stirring gently and pouring into jars. Seal.

*Makes about 10 cups (5 lb)*

### Plum Jam

*1 kg (2 lb) plums*              *4 cups (2 lb) sugar*
*¾ cup (6 fl oz) water*

Halve the plums and remove the stones (pits). Crack a few of the stones and remove the kernels. Put the fruit, kernels and water into a preserving pan. Bring to the boil, and simmer until the plums are soft, stirring frequently. Warm the sugar and add it to the plums, stirring until dissolved. Boil rapidly until setting point is reached. Skim. Pour into jars and seal.

*Makes about 7 cups (3½ lb)*

### Plum and Apple Jam

*1 kg (2 lb) plums,*              *Pinch of salt*
*slightly under-ripe*            *3–4 teaspoons lemon*
*1 kg (2 lb) cooking*                *juice*
*apples*                      *8 cups (4 lb) sugar*
*1 cup (8 fl oz) water*

Halve the plums and remove the stones (pits). Peel and core the apples and chop. Put the fruit into a preserving pan with the water and salt. Bring to the boil and simmer for 20 minutes or until soft. Add the lemon juice, then slowly add the sugar, stirring to dissolve. Boil rapidly for 40 minutes or until setting point is reached. Skim. Pour into jars. Seal.

*Makes about 14 cups (7 lb)*

———— ◆ ————

*Plums are equally delicious in spicy sauces
and sweet chutneys.*

## Plum and Orange Jam

| | |
|---|---|
| 1½ kg (3 lb) plums | 1¼ cups (10 fl oz) water |
| 2 oranges | 6 cups (3 lb) sugar |

Roughly chop the plums and put into a preserving pan. Grate the rind from the oranges, then squeeze the juice. Put the seeds in a muslin (cheesecloth) bag. Add the grated rind, juice, muslin bag and water to the pan. Bring to the boil and simmer gently until the plums are tender, then remove the bag of seeds. As the plum stones (pits) rise to the surface, remove with a slotted spoon.

Add the sugar and heat gently, stirring until the sugar has dissolved. Boil rapidly for about 15 minutes or until setting point is reached. Skim. Pour into jars and seal.

*Makes about 10 cups (5 lb)*

## Plum and Walnut Conserve

| | |
|---|---|
| 1 kg (2 lb) plums | Sugar |
| 100 g (4 oz) seedless | Juice of 1 lemon |
| dark raisins | 100 g (4 oz) walnuts, |
| 1 orange, thinly sliced, | chopped (diced) |
| seeds removed | |

Chop the plums, remove the stones (pits) and combine with the raisins and orange slices. Measure the fruit and add sugar equal to three-quarters of the amount. Put into a preserving pan and cook slowly for about 45 minutes, stirring frequently. Stir in the lemon juice and walnuts. Pour into jars and seal.

*Makes about 6 cups (3 lb)*

———— ◆ ————

*The Greeks dedicated the walnut to the Goddess Artemis (or Diana) and feasts in her honour were held under walnut trees.*

## Prune Conserve

500 g (1 lb) prunes,
   pitted
5 cups (40 fl oz) water
2 cups (1 lb) sugar

½ teaspoon ground
   cinnamon
Grated rind and
   juice of 1 lemon

Halve the prunes and soak overnight in the water. Transfer to a preserving pan, bring to the boil and simmer for about 20 minutes or until soft. Add the sugar gradually, stirring to dissolve. Mix in the cinnamon, lemon rind and juice, then boil rapidly until setting point is reached. Pour into jars and seal.

*Makes about 4 cups (2 lb)*

## Quince Jam

1 kg (2 lb) quinces,
   peeled, cored and
   finely chopped

5 cups (40 fl oz) water
Juice of 1 lemon
4 cups (2 lb) sugar

Put the quinces into a preserving pan. Add the water, bring to the boil and simmer gently until the fruit is tender—about 20 minutes. Add the lemon juice and sugar, stirring until the sugar has dissolved. Boil rapidly until setting point is reached. Skim. Pour into jars. Seal.

*Makes about 7 cups (3½ lb)*

———◆———

*The common quince is a native of Iran and Turkey and perhaps Greece and the Crimea. The name quince is derived from Crete, the Greek island where a variety of the plant was grown.*

### Pressure Cooker (Canner) Quince Jam

1 kg (2 lb) quinces
½ lemon
¾ cup (6 fl oz) water

3-4 teaspoons finely
   chopped (minced)
   fresh ginger (ginger root)
4 cups (2 lb) sugar

Peel, core and finely chop the quinces. Slice the lemon and tie the seeds in a muslin (cheesecloth) bag. Put the fruit and muslin bag into a pressure cooker with the water and ginger. Pressure cook for 15 minutes. Remove from the heat and when pressure reduces, remove the cover and discard the muslin bag. Add the sugar and bring mixture slowly to the boil, stirring to dissolve. Boil rapidly until setting point is reached. Skim. Allow to stand for 5 minutes before stirring gently and pouring into jars. Seal.

*Makes about 7 cups (3½ lb)*

### Raspberry Jam

1 kg (2 lb)
   raspberries
4 cups (2 lb) sugar
1 pinch salt

3-4 teaspoons lemon
   juice
1 teaspoon butter

Put the raspberries into a preserving pan and mash with a potato masher. Bring to the boil and simmer for a few minutes without water. Slowly add the sugar, stirring to dissolve. Add the salt and lemon juice. Boil rapidly for 5 minutes, then add the butter and stir until melted. Boil for another 2 minutes. Pour into jars. Cool and seal.

*Makes about 7 cups (3½ lb)*

## Strawberry Jam

| | |
|---|---|
| *1 kg (2 lb)*<br>    *strawberries* | *3 teaspoons lemon*<br>    *juice* |
| *4 cups (2 lb) sugar* | *Pinch of salt* |
| *3 teaspoons water* | *1 teaspoon butter* |

Hull the strawberries and put into a bowl with half the sugar and the water. Leave in the refrigerator for about 3 hours. Put into a preserving pan with the lemon juice and salt, and heat slowly until not quite at boiling point. Add the rest of the sugar and, stirring constantly, bring slowly to the boil. Boil rapidly, stirring occasionally, for 45 minutes or until setting point is reached. Stir in the butter. Remove from the heat and let stand for 5 minutes before stirring gently and pouring into jars. Seal when cool.

*Makes about 7 cups (3½ lb)*

## Rockmelon (Cantaloupe) Jam

2 kg (4 lb) diced rock-
   melon (cantaloupe)
½ teaspoon salt

Juice of 2 lemons
8 cups (4 lb) sugar

Put the rockmelon into a preserving pan with the salt, lemon juice and
1 cup (8 oz) of the sugar. Cover and cook gently for about 45 minutes,
stirring occasionally. Add a little water if it starts to stick. Add the
remaining sugar and cook for another 30 minutes with the lid off, stirring
frequently. Pour into jars and seal.

*Makes about 14 cups (7 lb)*

## Marrow (Summer Squash) and Ginger Jam

1 kg (2 lb) marrow
   (summer squash),
   peeled and finely
   diced
4 cups (2 lb) sugar

Juice of 2 lemons
3 tablespoons finely
   chopped (minced)
   preserved ginger

Bring some water to the boil, and simmer the marrow until tender. Drain
and put into a large bowl. Sprinkle over the sugar and leave the bowl,
loosely covered, in a warm place overnight so the sugar starts to dissolve.

Transfer the marrow and sugar to a preserving pan, add the lemon
juice and, over a low heat, finish dissolving the sugar. Add the ginger
and simmer, stirring occasionally, until setting point is reached. Leave
for 5 minutes. Stir gently and pour into jars. Seal.

*Makes about 7 cups (3½ lb)*

### Beetroot (Beet) Jam

An unusual jam that is good with cold roast lamb or pork in a sandwich.

| | |
|---|---|
| 1 kg (2 lb) beetroots (beets) | 2½ cups (20 fl oz) water |
| 500 g (1 lb) cooking apples | Juice of two lemons |
| | 6 cups (3 lb) sugar |

Bring a saucepan of water to the boil and cook beetroots (with a little of the stalk left on) for about 20 minutes or until tender. Drain, cool slightly, then chop off the stem, and peel. Set aside.

Peel, core and slice the apples and place in a preserving pan with the water and lemon juice. Put the peel, cores and seeds into a muslin (cheesecloth) bag and add to the pan. Cover and cook gently until the apples are soft.

Remove the bag and squeeze the juice into the pan. Use a potato masher to puree the apples, then grate (shred) the beetroots and add to the pan. Simmer for a few minutes, then add the sugar and keep on a low heat, stirring until the sugar has dissolved. Boil rapidly until setting point is reached. Skim. Pour into jars and seal.

*Makes about 10 cups (5 lb)*

### Rhubarb Jam

| | |
|---|---|
| 2 kg (4 lb) rhubarb, cut into 2.5 cm (1 inch) pieces | 1 cup (8 fl oz) water |
| | Juice of 1 lemon |
| | 6 cups (3 lb) sugar |

Put the rhubarb, water and lemon juice into a preserving pan. Bring to the boil and simmer until the rhubarb is soft. Add the sugar, stirring until dissolved, then boil rapidly until setting point is reached. Skim. Pour into jars and seal.

*Makes about 10 cups (5 lb)*

### Pumpkin (Winter Squash) and Orange Jam

*1 kg (2 lb) pumpkin*            *3 oranges*
   *(winter squash)*            *4 cups (2 lb) sugar*
*1 lemon*

Peel the pumpkin and remove the seeds. Cut into 2.5 cm (1 inch) cubes and simmer until tender. Drain and mash or puree the pumpkin in a food processor. Grate the rind and squeeze the juice from the lemon and oranges. Put the pumpkin, rind and juice into a pan, add the sugar and bring slowly to the boil, stirring to dissolve the sugar. Simmer for 20 minutes, stirring constantly, until thick. Pour into jars and seal.

*Makes about 7 cups (3½ lb)*

### Rose Jam

Surprise your friends with this rare treat. Try it on water biscuits (crackers) spread with cream cheese, or as a filling for a heavenly sponge cake.

*225 g (8 oz) rose*            *1 cup (8 fl oz) water*
   *petals*            *Juice of 1 lemon*
*1 cup (8 oz) sugar*            *Pinch of tartaric acid*

Cut off the white or green base of each petal—it has a bitter taste. Put the rose petals, sugar and water into a saucepan and bring to the boil, stirring to dissolve the sugar. Simmer until the sugar hardens on a wooden spoon, then add the lemon juice and tartaric acid. Pour into jars and seal when cool.

*Makes about 1½ cups (12 oz)*

———— ◆ ————

*Rose petals can be crystallised to make
an attractive garnish for icecreams and cakes.*

## Rose Conserve

This Indian delicacy is wonderful stirred into vanilla ice-cream or fruit drinks.

*225 g (8 oz) rose petals*          *3 cups (1½ lb) sugar*

Cut off the white or green base (it has a bitter taste) of each petal, then crush the petals finely with a mortar and pestle. Starting and ending with the sugar, layer sugar and crushed rose petals in a jar. Seal and leave in a sunny place until the sugar has melted—this will take several days. It is then ready to use.

*Makes about 3 cups (1½ lb)*

## Tomato Jam

Served with cream, this unusual jam makes a delicious dessert.

*1 kg (2 lb) sugar*          *1 kg (2 lb) tomatoes,*
*1 cup (8 fl oz) water*          *skinned and sliced*

Put the sugar and water into a preserving pan and bring to the boil, stirring to dissolve the sugar. Boil for 5 minutes, then add the tomatoes. Continue to boil, stirring frequently for about 40 minutes. Skim. Leave for 5 minutes, then pour into jars and seal.

*Makes about 7 cups (3½ lb)*

———— ◆ ————

*The tomato originated in South America*
*and was probably taken to Europe from*
*Mexico in the 16th century. It is now*
*a staple food of the Mediterranean region.*

## Green Tomato Jam

| | |
|---|---|
| *1 kg (2 lb) green tomatoes* | *½ teaspoon ground ginger* |
| *Grated rind, seeds and juice of 1 orange* | *3 cups (1½ lb) sugar* |

Skin the tomatoes (first plunge into boiling water to make it easier), then chop and put into a preserving pan. Add the orange rind, juice, seeds tied in a muslin (cheesecloth) bag, and ginger. Bring slowly to the boil.

Simmer for about an hour, stirring occasionally, until the tomatoes are pulpy. Remove the muslin bag, then stir in the sugar and dissolve over a low heat. Boil rapidly for 15 minutes or until setting point is reached. Skim, and pour into jars. Seal.

*Makes about 5 cups (2½ lb)*

### Green Tomato and Banana Jam

1 kg (2 lb) green
   tomatoes
6 bananas

3–4 teaspoons
   preserved ginger
2 lemons
4 cups (2 lb) sugar

Slice the tomatoes, peel and slice bananas, chop the ginger, and grate the lemon rind. Set aside the lemons. Put the tomatoes, bananas, ginger and grated lemon rind into a preserving pan, cover with sugar and let stand for 12 hours. Squeeze the juice from the lemons and add it to the pan. Boil rapidly until setting point is reached. Skim. Pour into jars and seal.

*Makes about 7 cups (3½ lb)*


### Marie's Tomato and Pineapple Jam

2 kg (4 lb) tomatoes
Salt
1 small pineapple,
   peeled, cored and
   grated (shredded)

6 cups (3 lb) sugar
Juice of 2 lemons

Skin the tomatoes (plunge into boiling water first) then chop, sprinkle with salt and leave in the refrigerator overnight.

Drain the tomatoes and put into a preserving pan with the grated pineapple. Bring to the boil and simmer until soft and pulpy. Add the warmed sugar, stirring until dissolved, then boil rapidly for 30 minutes. Add lemon juice and pour into jars. Seal.

*Makes about 10 cups (5 lb)*

## Christmas Jam

This jam is ideal for making mince pies and slices.

1 kg (2 lb) cooking
apples
Juice and grated rind
of 1 grapefruit
100 g (4 oz) shredded
lemon peel
3-4 teaspoons
chopped, preserved
ginger

500 g (1 lb) sultanas
(golden raisins)
½ teaspoon ground
nutmeg
5 cups (40 fl oz)
water
2 cups (1 lb) sugar
1 teaspoon almond
essence (extract)

Peel, core and slice the apples and put into a preserving pan with the grapefruit rind and juice, lemon peel, preserved ginger, sultanas, nutmeg and water. Bring slowly to the boil and simmer until the apples are soft. Add the sugar, stirring to dissolve. Boil rapidly for 15 minutes, stirring occasionally. Add the almond essence and pour into bottles. Seal.

*Makes about 8 cups (4 lb)*

# $\mathcal{J}$ELLIES

G lowing, translucent jellies take time to make but the results are worth it. With a wide range of sweet and savoury applications, they are one of the most versatile of preserves.

The difference between jams and jellies is that, in jellies, only the juice of the fruit is used in the final product: a clear, translucent jelly that holds its shape when spooned on to a plate. If this seems wasteful don't discard the pulp—use it to make a delicious fruit butter (see page 70).

## Jelly Bag

Jelly bags are available at kitchenware, homeware and specialty shops— if you plan on making a lot of jellies it's a good idea to buy one. But you can also improvise without going to any expense. You will need a square of porous cloth such as unbleached muslin (cheesecloth), calico, a piece of sheeting or a tea towel. It should be scalded before using and damp when used.

Turn a stool upside down or stand one chair upside down on another chair (with seat resting on seat). Tie the cloth securely to the legs of the stool or chair, so it dips loosely in the centre. Stand a bowl under the cloth. Pour the fruit pulp into the bag and allow the juice to strain through unaided into the bowl. Do not squeeze the cloth or push the fruit through or jelly may be cloudy. If handling only a small quantity of fruit pulp, you can simply line a colander with a cloth and use that as a jelly bag.

## Basic method

1. Choose the fruit, or a combination of fruits, with the correct balance of pectin and acid (see page 2). You can make certain types of jam using low pectin fruit, but not jelly.
2. Wash the fruit and remove any bruised or damaged parts.
3. Chop the fruit including the skin, seeds and stalks. The skin and seeds are often rich in pectin.
4. Put into a preserving pan and barely cover with water.
5. Cook until soft and pulpy.
6. Pour fruit pulp into a jelly bag which has been scalded first by pouring boiling water through it. It should be damp as a dry bag will absorb too much of the valuable fruit juice.
7. Leave to strain into a bowl overnight (or about 12 hours). Do not squeeze the bag or push the pulp through or it will make a cloudy jelly. (If using a high pectin fruit, such as redcurrants, you can increase the yield by allowing the juice to drip through for about an hour, then returning the pulp to the saucepan with half the quantity of water used in the original cooking. The pulp is simmered again then returned to the jelly bag to strain overnight into the bowl with the first lot of juice.) If clarity isn't a priority you can also speed up the process by straining pulp through a colander, using a wooden spoon to extract as much juice as possible, then straining the juice through a jelly bag into a bowl.
8. Measure the juice back into the preserving pan, then take a sample and test for pectin (see page 2).
9. Add sugar depending on pectin content. If high in pectin add 2 cups (1 lb) sugar for every 2½ cups (20 fl oz) juice, if medium in pectin add 1½ cups (12 oz) sugar for every 2½ cups (20 fl oz) juice.
10. Bring quickly to the boil, stirring to dissolve the sugar—make sure that all sugar has dissolved before reaching boiling point.
11. Boil rapidly, without stirring, until setting point is reached. Test for set after 10 minutes (see page 4).
12. Skim.
13. Using a ladle and heat-proof jug, pour into jars immediately.
14. Cover immediately with screw-top lids or waxed paper circles.

15. Label and store in a cool dark place.
16. When opened, keep in fridge.

*Yield:* You should get approximately 2½ kg (5 lb) jelly to every 6 cups (3 lb) sugar used.

## Apple Jelly

Cooking apples       Sugar
Water

Chop the whole apples and put into a preserving pan with barely enough water to cover. Bring to the boil and simmer gently for about 1 hour. Pour into a jelly bag and strain overnight. Do not press the fruit or bag but allow the juice to strain through unaided into a bowl.

Measure the juice back into the preserving pan and allow 2 cups (1 lb) sugar for every 2½ cups (20 fl oz) juice. Slowly bring to the boil, stirring until the sugar has dissolved. Boil rapidly until setting point is reached. Skim and pour into jars. Seal.

## Pressure Cooker (Canner) Apple and Rosemary Jelly

1 kg (2 lb) cooking       3½ cups (28 fl oz) water
    apples       Sugar
6 sprigs fresh rosemary

Chop the apples, peel and core included, and put them into a pressure cooker with the rosemary. Add the water, cover and pressure cook for 5 minutes. Remove from the heat and when the pressure drops, remove the lid and pour the pulp into a jelly bag. Allow it to strain through into a bowl overnight. Do not press the fruit or squeeze the bag.

Next day, measure the juice back into the cooker, adding 2 cups (1 lb) sugar to every 2½ cups (20 fl oz) juice. Bring slowly to the boil, uncovered, and stirring to dissolve the sugar. Boil rapidly, without stirring, until setting point is reached. Skim. Pour into jars and seal.

### Thyme Apple Jelly

This is a quickly-made jelly using store-bought fruit juice. I've tried making jellies with all sorts of bought fruit juice and find it almost impossible to achieve a good set—the result isn't wasted though, because I end up with a syrup that is excellent for basting roast meat. This recipe solves the problem by using commercial fruit pectin, which you can buy at health food shops and some supermarkets. You can adapt the recipe to other juices and flavours.

*2 cups (16 fl oz)*
*apple juice*
*4 teaspoons dried*
*thyme (or about 6–8*
*teaspoons of finely*
*chopped (minced)*
*fresh thyme)*

*50 g (2 oz) powdered*
*fruit pectin*
*1½ cups (12 oz) sugar*
*3 teaspoons lemon*
*juice*

Put the apple juice and thyme into a preserving pan and bring to the boil. Remove from the heat and leave for 1 hour. Strain, then stir in the powdered pectin, and return to the boil. Add the sugar and lemon juice, stirring to dissolve, then boil rapidly for 2 minutes, still stirring. Skim. Pour into jars and seal.

### Crab Apple Jelly

*Crab apples*
*Water*

*Sugar*

Cut the crab apples into quarters, put into a preserving pan with barely enough water to cover, and cook until pulpy. Strain through a jelly bag overnight. Do not press the fruit or bag, but allow the juice to strain through unaided into a bowl.

Measure the juice back into the preserving pan adding 2 cups (1 lb) sugar for every 2½ cups (20 fl oz) juice. Stir in the sugar and dissolve over a gentle heat, then boil rapidly until setting point is reached. Skim and pour into jars. Seal.

## Apple Jelly with Pineapple

| Cooking apples | Fresh or canned |
| --- | --- |
| Water | pineapple, finely |
| Sugar | chopped (minced) and |
| | drained—about 100 g |
| | (4 oz) for every 1 kg |
| | (2 lb) apples |

Chop the apples and put into a preserving pan (including cores and seeds) with barely enough water to cover. Bring to the boil and simmer ʒently for about 1 hour. Pour into a jelly bag and strain overnight. Do not press the fruit or bag but allow the juice to strain through unaided into a bowl.

Measure the juice back into the preserving pan and allow 2 cups (1 lb) sugar for every 2½ cups (20 fl oz) juice. Slowly bring to the boil, stirring until the sugar has dissolved. Boil rapidly for 10 minutes, then add the pineapple. Continue boiling until setting point is reached. Skim and allow to stand for 5 minutes before pouring into jars. Seal.

## Marjoram Jelly

| 500 g (1 lb) cooking | Peeled rind, juice |
| --- | --- |
| apples | and seeds of 1 lemon |
| Bunch of sweet | Water |
| marjoram | Sugar |

Roughly chop the apples and put into a preserving pan (peel and core included) with the sweet marjoram, lemon rind, juice and seeds, and barely enough water to cover. Cook until pulpy. Strain through a jelly bag overnight. Do not press the fruit or bag, but allow the juice to strain through unaided into a bowl.

Measure juice back into the preserving pan adding 2 cups (1 lb) sugar for every 2½ cups (20 fl oz) juice. Stir in the sugar and dissolve over a gentle heat. Boil rapidly until setting point is reached. Skim and pour into jars.

## Rosemary Jelly

| | |
|---|---|
| 2 kg (4 lb) cooking apples, sliced | 4 tablespoons fresh rosemary leaves |
| 2½ cups (20 fl oz) water | 1 cup (8 fl oz) malt vinegar |
| | Sugar |

Put the apples (peel, cores and seeds included) and water into a preserving pan with half of the rosemary. Bring to the boil and simmer until the fruit is pulpy. Add the vinegar and simmer for another 5 minutes. Pour the pulp into a jelly bag and allow the juice to strain into a bowl overnight. Do not push the fruit or squeeze the bag.

Measure the juice into the preserving pan, adding 2 cups (1 lb) sugar to every 2½ cups (20 fl oz) of juice. Bring slowly to the boil, stirring to dissolve the sugar. Boil rapidly, without stirring, until setting point is reached. Skim. Stir the remaining rosemary into the jelly. Pour into jars and seal.

## Rose Geranium Jelly

| | |
|---|---|
| Cooking apples | Rose Geranium (Pelargonium) |
| Water | leaves—4 for every |
| Sugar | 1 kg (2 lb) apples |

Chop the apples and put into a preserving pan (including peel and cores) with barely enough water to cover. Bring to the boil and simmer gently for about 1 hour. Pour into a jelly bag and strain overnight. Do not press the fruit or bag but allow the juice to strain through unaided into a bowl.

Measure the juice back into the preserving pan and allow 2 cups (1 lb) sugar for every 2½ cups (20 fl oz) juice. Tie the rose geranium leaves in a muslin (cheesecloth) bag and add to the pan. Bring to the boil slowly, stirring until the sugar has dissolved. Boil rapidly until setting point is reached. Remove the muslin bag. Skim, and pour into jars. If you like, suspend 1 fresh rose geranium leaf in each jar of hot jelly. Seal.

## Mint Jelly

| | |
|---|---|
| 1½ kg (3 lb) cooking apples | Sugar |
| 2½ cups (20 fl oz) water | Few drops green food colouring |
| Bunch of fresh mint | 3 tablespoons chopped fresh mint leaves |
| 2½ cups (20 fl oz) white vinegar | |

Chop the apples roughly (including peel and core) and put into a preserving pan with the water and bunch of mint. Simmer until soft and pulpy. Add the vinegar, bring to the boil, and simmer for 5 minutes. Pour into a jelly bag and leave to strain into a bowl overnight. Do not squeeze or press the bag.

Measure the juice back into the preserving pan adding 2 cups (1 lb) sugar for every 2½ cups (20 fl oz) juice. Bring to the boil, stirring to dissolve the sugar. Boil rapidly until setting point is reached. Skim. Add the colouring and chopped (minced) mint leaves, and leave for 5 minutes before stirring gently and pouring into jars. Seal.

## Grape Jelly

Citric acid is sometimes used as a substitute for lemon juice when making jams and jellies with low-acid fruit.

|  |  |
|---|---|
| 2 kg (4 lb) white | 1 cup (8 fl oz) water |
| (green) or black | Sugar |
| (red) grapes | 1 teaspoon citric acid |

Put the grapes into a preserving pan with the water. Bring to the boil and simmer gently for about 15 minutes, mashing the fruit with a wooden spoon or potato masher. Pour into a jelly bag and allow to strain into a bowl overnight. Do not press the fruit or squeeze the bag.

Measure the juice back into the preserving pan, adding 1½ cups (12 oz) sugar for every 2½ cups (20 fl oz) juice. Add the citric acid. Bring slowly to the boil, stirring to dissolve the sugar, then boil rapidly, without stirring, until setting point is reached. Skim. Pour the jelly into jars and seal.

## Blackcurrant and Raspberry Jelly

|  |  |
|---|---|
| 1 kg (2 lb) black- | 2½ cups (20 fl oz) |
| currants | water |
| 1 kg (2 lb) | Sugar |
| raspberries |  |

Put the blackcurrants and raspberries into a preserving pan with the water, bring to the boil and simmer gently until the fruit is tender. Mash with a potato masher. Pour the juice and pulp into a jelly bag and leave to strain overnight into a bowl. Do not press the fruit or squeeze the bag.

Measure the juice back into the preserving pan and add 2 cups (1 lb) sugar for every 2½ cups (20 fl oz) strained juice. Bring to the boil, stirring to dissolve the sugar. Boil rapidly until setting point is reached. Skim. Pour into jars and seal.

## Blackcurrant Jelly

*1 kg (2 lb) black-*      *2½ cups (20 fl oz) water*
*currants*           *Sugar*

Put the blackcurrants into a preserving pan with the water, bring to the boil and simmer gently until the fruit is tender. Mash with a potato masher. Pour the juice and pulp into a jelly bag and leave to strain overnight into a bowl. Do not press the fruit or squeeze the bag.

Measure the juice back into the preserving pan and add 2 cups (1 lb) sugar for every 2½ cups (20 fl oz) strained juice. Bring to the boil, stirring to dissolve the sugar, then boil rapidly until setting point is reached. Skim. Pour into jars and seal.

## Spiced Grape Jelly

2 kg (4 lb) white      1 cup (8 fl oz) water
  (green) or black      Sugar
  (red) grapes      1 teaspoon citric acid
2 cinnamon sticks

Mash the grapes with a potato masher and put into a preserving pan with the cinnamon sticks and water. Bring to the boil and simmer gently until the fruit is soft and pulpy. Pour into a jelly bag and strain into a bowl overnight. Do not press the fruit or squeeze the bag.

Measure the juice back into the preserving pan, adding 1½ cups (12 oz) sugar for every 2½ cups (20 fl oz) juice. Bring slowly to the boil, stirring to dissolve the sugar. Boil rapidly, without stirring, until setting point is reached. Skim. Pour the jelly into the jars and seal.

## Guava Jelly

1 kg (2 lb) guavas      2 lemons
1 green apple      Sugar

Chop the guavas, apple and lemons. Put the fruit into a preserving pan with barely enough water to cover. Bring to the boil and simmer for 45 minutes or until the fruit is very soft. Mash the fruit with a potato masher, then pour the pulp into a jelly bag and leave to strain into a bowl overnight. Do not press the fruit or squeeze the bag.

Measure the juice back into the preserving pan and allow 2 cups (1 lb) sugar to every 2½ cups (20 fl oz) juice. Bring to the boil, stirring to dissolve the sugar. Boil rapidly, without stirring, until setting point is reached. Skim. Pour into jars and seal.

——— ◆ ———

*The whole fruit of guava is edible, although it is usually peeled and can be eaten fresh or stewed.*

## Wine Jelly

This beautiful jelly is delicious with cold roast veal or pork.

1½ kg (3 lb) black
(red) grapes,
crushed (minced)
1¼ cups (10 fl oz) red
wine
700 g (1½ lb) quinces,
sliced

1 lemon, thinly
sliced
6 cardamom seeds
Sugar
¾ cup (6 fl oz) brandy

Put the grapes and wine into a preserving pan and bring to the boil. Simmer for 20-30 minutes, or until the fruit is pulpy. Add the quinces (cores and seeds included), lemon and cardamom seeds, and continue simmering for 20-30 minutes until the quinces are pulpy. Pour the contents of the pan into a jelly bag and allow the juice to strain into a bowl overnight. Do not press the fruit or squeeze the bag.

Measure the juice and pour it into the preserving pan adding 2 cups (1 lb) sugar to every 2½ cups (20 fl oz) juice. Bring slowly to the boil, stirring to dissolve the sugar. Add the brandy and boil rapidly, without stirring, until setting point is reached. Skim. Pour the jelly into jars and seal.

## Pressure Cooker (Canner) Orange Jelly

1 kg (2 lb) Seville
(bitter) oranges
1 lemon

3½ cups (28 fl oz)
water
Sugar

Chop the oranges and lemon, and put the fruit into a pressure cooker. Add the water, cover and pressure cook for 15 minutes. When the pressure drops, remove the lid and pour the pulp into a jelly bag and leave to strain into a bowl overnight. Do not press the fruit or squeeze the bag.

Measure the juice back into the cooker, adding 2 cups (1 lb) sugar to every 2½ cups (20 fl oz) juice. Bring slowly to the boil, uncovered, and stirring to dissolve the sugar. Boil rapidly, without stirring, until setting point is reached. Skim. Pour into jars and seal.

## Quince Jelly

1 kg (2 lb) quinces
7½ cups (60 fl oz) water

½ cup (4 fl oz) lemon juice
Sugar

Chop the whole quinces and put into a preserving pan with the water and lemon juice. Bring to the boil and simmer, covered, for 1 hour or until the fruit is very soft. Pour into a jelly bag and leave to strain overnight. Do not press the fruit or squeeze the bag, but allow the juice to strain through unaided into a bowl.

Measure the juice and allow 2 cups (1 lb) sugar for every 2½ cups (20 fl oz) juice. Return the juice and sugar to the preserving pan. Bring to the boil, stirring until the sugar has dissolved. Boil rapidly until setting point is reached. Skim. Pour into jars. Seal.

## Redcurrant Jelly

A classic accompaniment to roast lamb. In this recipe the fruit pulp is simmered with water twice to increase the yield of juice. This method can only be used with fruit that is rich in pectin.

1 kg (2 lb) red-currants

3¾ cups (30 fl oz) water
Sugar

Put the redcurrants and 2½ cups (20 fl oz) of the water into a preserving pan and bring slowly to the boil while mashing with a potato masher. Simmer until the redcurrants are soft and pulpy. Pour into a jelly bag and leave to strain into a bowl for about 1 hour.

Return the pulp to the preserving pan with the rest of the water and simmer again for about 20 minutes. Pour into the jelly bag and leave to strain overnight into the bowl with the first lot of juice. Do not squeeze the bag.

Measure the juice into the preserving pan and add 2 cups (1 lb) sugar for every 2½ cups (20 fl oz) juice. Bring to the boil, stirring to dissolve the sugar. Boil rapidly until setting point is reached. Skim. Pour into jars and seal.

### Red Pepper Jelly

A delicious and interesting accompaniment to cold roast meat.

*9 red capsicums
 (peppers), seeds and
 stems removed
1½ cups (12 oz) sugar
½ cup (4 fl oz) cider
 vinegar*

*1 banana chilli
 (yellow wax
 peppers), seeds
 and stem removed
 (optional)*

Put all ingredients into a food processor and mince. Transfer to a saucepan and bring slowly to the boil, stirring to dissolve the sugar. Simmer until the mixture thickens, about 20–30 minutes. Pour into jars and seal.

### *Rhubarb Jelly*

Delicious with char-grilled lamb cutlets or chops.

| | |
|---|---|
| *1 kg (2 lb)* | *1½ cups (10 fl oz) water* |
| *rhubarb stalks* | *Sugar* |

Chop the rhubarb stalks into short lengths, put into a preserving pan with water, and cook until soft and pulpy. Pour into a jelly bag and leave to strain into a bowl overnight. Do not squeeze the bag.

Measure the juice back into the preserving pan and add 1½ cups (12½oz) sugar to every 2½ cups (20 fl oz) juice. Bring to the boil, stirring to dissolve the sugar, then boil rapidly until setting point is reached. Skim. Pour into jars and seal.

# $\mathcal{M}$ARMALADES

The word 'marmalade' derives from 'marmelo', the Portuguese word for quince; the original marmalade was a quince paste. A more romantic interpretation of the name's origin dates back to the reign of Mary Queen of Scots. Whenever the Queen was sick she asked for an orange preserve that she had enjoyed in her early life in France. It became known as 'Marie-malade'. Many Scots claim that the modern name is a corruption of these words. The Scottish connection certainly goes back a long way. It was the Scottish Keiller family who made the first commercial marmalade as we know it.

Marmalades are made from citrus fruits, sometimes combined with another fruit or even a vegetable. Slices of fruit or rind are suspended in a translucent jelly—marmalades are related more closely to jellies than jam. The flavour is sharp as well as sweet; the perfect accompaniment to breakfast toast! But there are almost as many ways of eating it as there are of making it.

## Basic method

1. Wash and, if necessary, scrub the fruit with a small brush.
2. Plunge the fruit into boiling water for about 2 minutes—this makes it easier to remove the rind.
3. Peel the rind and cut into thin or thick shreds, as desired. If making a chunky marmalade, cut off the pith with the rind, otherwise cut

the pith off after the rind and set aside. Like the seeds, the pith is a valuable source of pectin and should be utilised.

4. Put the rind into the preserving pan with half the water specified in the recipe (usually about 5 cups [40 fl oz] water to 500 g [1 lb] fruit) and simmer for 1–1½ hours or until the rind is tender.

5. Chop the rest of the fruit—do this on a plate rather than a board so that none of the juice is wasted. Put chopped fruit and juice into a saucepan with the seeds and the rest of the water. Simmer for 1–1½ hours while the rind is cooking.

6. Strain the liquid from the saucepan into the preserving pan, then separate the fruit pulp from the pith and coarse tissue (membrane), and add it to the preserving pan. Discard seeds, pith and coarse tissue.

7. Add sugar, stirring to dissolve.

8. Boil rapidly until setting point is reached (see page 4). Test for set after 10 minutes—it usually takes 15–20 minutes.

9. Skim.

10. Leave to stand for 5–10 minutes, then stir gently before pouring into jars. This stops the rind from rising in the jar.

11. Seal.

12. Label and store in a cool dark place.

There are many variations on this method—often the pith and seeds are tied in a muslin (cheesecloth) bag and cooked with the rind, then lifted out before sugar is added. Some traditional recipes call for soaking the fruit overnight, but there doesn't seem to be any great advantage to this.

NOTE: *You can make an excellent sauce for steamed puddings or ice-cream by bringing 1 cup (8 oz) marmalade and ½ cup (4 oz) of wine, brandy, or whisky to the boil and straining it through a sieve. Serve hot with puddings or cold with ice-cream.*

### Cumquat (Kumquat) Marmalade

Soaking fruit overnight is a marmalade-making tradition that seems unnecessary. An alternative is to soak the fruit in boiling water for 1 hour to soften the skin and decrease the cooking time.

*1 kg (2 lb) cumquats*      *Juice of 2 lemons*
*(kumquats)*      *6 cups (3 lb) sugar*
*10 cups (80 fl oz)*
*boiling water*

Cut the cumquats into thin slices, cover with boiling water and leave to stand for 1 hour. Bring the fruit to the boil, then simmer until tender. Add the lemon juice and sugar, and stir until the sugar has dissolved. Boil rapidly until setting point is reached. Skim. Allow to stand for 5 minutes before stirring gently and pouring into jars. Seal.

*Makes about 10 cups (5 lb)*

## Choko (Christophene, Chayote) and Lemon Marmalade

If you have chokos growing in your garden, you will know what a problem it can be to find enough ways to use the crop from this prolific vine. Try this unusual marmalade.

12 chokos
(christophenes,
chayote)
Juice of 4 lemons
1¾ kg (3½ lb) sugar
1 cup water

Finely shredded rind
of 4 lemons
6–8 teaspoons finely
chopped (minced)
preserved ginger

Peel and dice the chokos—wear gloves (or remove the peel under running water)— because the juices can affect sensitive skin. Sprinkle with lemon juice and 1 cup (½ lb) of the sugar, and leave overnight.

Put into a preserving pan with the water, shredded rind and preserved ginger. Bring to the boil and simmer gently until the chokos and lemon rind are soft—about 45 minutes. Add the rest of the sugar, stirring to dissolve. Boil rapidly until setting point is reached. Leave for 10 minutes before stirring gently and pouring into jars. Seal.

*Makes about 10 cups (5 lb)*

## Four Fruit Marmalade

1 grapefruit
1 orange
1 lemon

1 pineapple
10 cups (80 fl oz) water
Sugar

Cut the grapefruit, orange and lemon into thin slices and then into segments, reserving the seeds. Shred the pineapple. Put all the fruit and water into a preserving pan with the seeds tied in a muslin (cheesecloth) bag, and bring slowly to the boil. Simmer for 1½ hours or until reduced by about half. Remove the muslin bag.

Measure the pulp and add 1½ cups (12 oz) sugar for every cup (8 oz) pulp. Bring to the boil, stirring to dissolve the sugar. Boil rapidly until setting point is reached. Skim. Leave for 10 minutes before stirring gently and pouring into jars. Seal.

*Makes about 10 cups (5 lb)*

## Grapefruit Marmalade

*1 kg (2 lb) grapefuit*          *15 cups (120 fl oz) water*
*3 lemons*                       *12 cups (6 lb) sugar*

Wash the grapefruit in hot water, then remove the peel, cut into thin strips and put into a preserving pan. Halve the grapefruit, squeeze out the juice, remove the seeds and reserve them. Add the juice to the preserving pan. Cut the pith off the fruit and reserve. Chop the grapefruit and add it to the pan. Squeeze the juice from the lemons and add it to the pan, reserving the seeds. Slice the lemons and tie in a muslin (cheesecloth) bag with the lemon seeds, grapefruit seeds and grapefruit pith. Add to the pan with the water. Bring to the boil and simmer for 2 hours or until the grapefruit peel is tender. Remove the bag and squeeze any juice into the pan. Add the sugar, stirring until dissolved. Boil rapidly until setting point is reached. Skim. Leave for 10 minutes before stirring gently and pouring into jars. Seal.

*Makes about 20 cups (10 lb)*

◆

*The name grapefruit comes from the*
*tendency of the fruit to hang in clusters.*

## Pressure Cooker (Canner) Grapefruit Marmalade

| | |
|---|---|
| 6 oranges | Water |
| 6 small grapefruit | Sugar |
| 2 lemons | |

Slice the oranges, grapefruit and lemons finely. Remove the seeds and tie in a muslin (cheesecloth) bag. Measure the fruit in a measuring jug and put into a pressure cooker with 900 ml (30 fl oz) water for every 600 ml (20 fl oz) fruit, and the bag of seeds. Pressure cook for 15 minutes. Remove from the heat, and when pressure reduces, remove the lid. Remove muslin bag.

Measure pulp and add an equal amount of sugar. Leave lid off pressure cooker and bring to the boil, stirring to dissolve the sugar. Boil rapidly for 15 minutes or until setting point is reached. Skim. Allow to stand 10 minutes before stirring gently and pouring into jars. Seal.

*Makes about 20 cups (10 lb)*


## Lemon Marmalade

| | |
|---|---|
| 1½ kg (3 lb) lemons | 12 cups (6 lb) sugar |
| 15 cups (120 fl oz) water | |

Wash the lemons in hot water, then cut the rind off as thinly as possible and shred—thin or thick as desired—and put into a preserving pan with half the water. Chop the lemon flesh and put into another saucepan with the rest of the water.

Bring both pans to the boil and simmer for 2 hours or until the lemon rind is tender. Strain the liquid from the saucepan into the preserving pan. Separate the fruit pulp from the pith and coarse tissue, and add it to the preserving pan. Add the sugar and bring to the boil, stirring until the sugar has dissolved. Boil rapidly until setting point is reached. Skim. Allow to stand for 10 minutes before stirring gently and pouring into jars. Seal.

*Makes about 14 cups (7 lb)*

### Mint and Lemon Marmalade

A superb accompaniment to lamb—either grilled (broiled) or roasted.

8 lemons
2 oranges
2½ cups (20 fl oz)
    cider vinegar
1½ cups (12 oz) sugar

½ teaspoon salt
1/3 cup finely
    chopped (minced)
    fresh mint leaves

Thinly peel the rind from the lemons and oranges, cut into thin slivers and put into a preserving pan. Squeeze the lemons and oranges, and add the juice to the pan. Tie the seeds in a muslin (cheesecloth) bag and add to the pan. Add cider vinegar and bring to the boil, then leave it to simmer for 1 hour.

Remove the muslin bag. Add the sugar and salt, stirring to dissolve, then boil rapidly until setting point is reached. Skim. Add the chopped mint and leave for 10 minutes before stirring gently and pouring into jars. Seal.

*Makes about 2½ cups (1¼ lb)*

NOTE: *Refrigerate after opening.*

### Pressure Cooker (Canner) Lemon Marmalade

4 lemons                          1 grapefruit
5 cups (40 fl oz) water           Sugar

Thinly peel the lemons, cut the rind into thin slivers and put into the pressure cooker with 1½ cups (12 fl oz) of the water. Cover and pressure cook for 10 minutes. When pressure drops, transfer the lemon peel and liquid to a bowl.

Chop the lemons and grapefruit, and put them into the cooker with the rest of the water. Cover and pressure cook for 15 minutes. When the pressure drops, pour the pulp into a jelly bag. Add most of the liquid from the lemon peel, but retain enough liquid to keep the peel moist. Leave to strain overnight into a bowl. Do not press the fruit or squeeze the bag.

Measure the liquid back into the cooker, adding 2 cups (1 lb) sugar to every 2½ cups (20 fl oz) juice. Add the lemon peel. Bring to the boil, uncovered, stirring to dissolve the sugar. Boil rapidly, without stirring, until setting point is reached. Skim. Allow to stand for 10 minutes, then pour into jars. Seal when cool.

*Makes about 7 cups (3½ lb)*

### Mandarin (Tangerine) Marmalade (1)

I don't know why mandarins (tangerines) aren't used as often as other citrus fruits in marmalade. They make a delicious and unusual preserve.

7 mandarins                   1 lemon
 (tangerines)                 4 cups (2 lb) sugar
 (preferably with             4 cups (32 fl oz)
 thin, tight skins)            boiling water

Slice the mandarins and lemon thinly. Remove the seeds and pour ½ cup (4 fl oz) boiling water over them and let stand for 1 hour. Pour the remaining boiling water over the mandarin and lemon slices and let stand for 1 hour.

Put the fruit into a preserving pan, and strain water from seeds into it. Simmer for 1 hour or until the skins are soft. Add the warmed sugar (see page 4), stirring to dissolve. Boil rapidly until mixture begins to clear, then reduce heat slightly and continue cooking until setting point is reached. Skim. Leave for 10 minutes before pouring into jars. Seal.

*Makes about 7 cups (3½ lb)*

## Mandarin (Tangerine) Marmalade (2)

| | |
|---|---|
| 7 mandarins (tangerines) (preferably with a thin, tight skin) | 4 cups (2 lb) sugar |
| | Juice of 1 lemon |
| | Juice of 1 orange |
| 4 cups (32 fl oz) boiling water | |

Slice the mandarins thinly. Remove the seeds and pour ½ cup (4 fl oz) boiling water over them and let stand for 1 hour. Pour remaining boiling water over the mandarin slices and let stand for 1 hour. Put the fruit into a preserving pan, and strain water from seeds into it.

Simmer for 1 hour or until the skins are soft. Add the warmed sugar, stirring to dissolve. Boil rapidly for 15 minutes, then add the lemon and orange juice, and continue cooking until setting point is reached. Skim. Leave for 10 minutes before pouring into jars. Seal.

*Makes about 7 cups (3½ lb)*

## Lime Marmalade

1½ kg (3 lb) limes              12 cups (6 lb) sugar
15 cups (120 fl oz)
   water

Wash the limes in hot water, then remove the rind, cut into thin strips and put into a preserving pan. Thinly slice the limes, cut slices into quarters, reserving the seeds, and add lime slices to the pan. Tie the seeds in a muslin (cheesecloth) bag and add to the pan with the water. Bring to the boil and simmer until the peel is tender. Remove the muslin bag and squeeze any juice into the pan. Add the sugar, stirring until dissolved. Boil rapidly until setting point is reached. Skim. Leave for 10 minutes before stirring gently and pouring it into jars. Seal.

*Makes about 16 cups (8 lb)*

## Rum and Lime Marmalade

1½ kg (3 lb) limes              10 cups (5 lb) sugar
10 cups (80 fl oz)             ½ cup (4 fl oz) white
   boiling water                 (light) rum

Slice the limes thinly and tie the seeds in a muslin (cheesecloth) bag. Put the sliced limes and muslin bag in a bowl, cover with the boiling water and leave overnight.

Transfer ingredients to a preserving pan and bring to the boil. Simmer until the rind is soft. Remove the muslin bag. Add the sugar, stirring to dissolve. Boil rapidly until setting point is reached. Add the rum and cook for another 5 minutes. Leave for 10 minutes before stirring gently and pouring into jars. Seal when cool.

*Makes about 14 cups (7 lb)*

———— ◆ ————

*Rum is actually distilled sugarcane and was invented by the early Spanish settlers of the West Indies.*

## Seville (Bitter) Orange Marmalade

1½ kg (3 lb) Seville          Juice of 2 lemons
  (bitter) oranges          12 cups (6 lb) sugar
15 cups (120 fl oz) water

Wash the oranges in hot water, then remove the peel as thinly as possible and cut into shreds—thin or thick as desired—and put into a preserving pan. Squeeze the oranges and strain the juice into the preserving pan. Reserve the seeds. Scrape out the pulp and add it to the pan, reserving the pith. Tie the seeds and pith in a muslin (cheesecloth) bag and add it to the preserving pan with the water and lemon juice.

Bring to the boil and simmer for 2 hours or until the orange peel is tender. Remove the muslin bag and squeeze over the preserving pan to extract any juice. Add the sugar, stirring until dissolved. Boil rapidly until setting point is reached. Skim. Allow to stand for 10 minutes before pouring into jars. Seal.

*Makes about 20 cups (10 lb)*

## Dark Orange Marmalade

1½ kg (3 lb) Seville          Juice of 2 lemons
  (bitter) oranges          12 cups (6 lb) sugar
15 cups (120 fl oz)          3 teaspoons molasses
  water

Wash the oranges in hot water, then remove the peel as thinly as possible, and cut into shreds—thin or thick as desired—and put into a preserving pan. Squeeze the oranges and strain the juice into the pan. Tie the seeds, pith and pulp in a muslin (cheesecloth) bag and add to the pan with the water and lemon juice.

Bring to the boil and simmer for 2 hours or until the orange peel is tender. Remove the muslin bag and squeeze the juice back into the pan. Add the sugar and molasses, stirring until dissolved. Boil rapidly until setting point is reached. Skim. Allow to stand for 10 minutes before stirring gently and pouring into jars. Seal.

*Makes about 20 cups (10 lb)*

## Pressure Cooker (Canner) Orange Marmalade

| Seville (bitter) oranges | Lemons Sugar |
|---|---|

Slice the oranges and lemons (6 oranges to 1 lemon), finely or thickly according to taste. Remove seeds and tie in a muslin (cheesecloth) bag. Measure the sliced fruit in a measuring jug, then put into a pressure cooker with an equal quantity of water and the bag of seeds. Make sure the pan is not more than half full. Cover and pressure cook for 15 minutes. Remove from the heat and when pressure reduces, remove the lid. Discard the muslin bag.

Measure the pulp and add an equal amount of sugar. Leave the lid off the pressure cooker and bring to the boil, stirring to dissolve the sugar. Boil rapidly for 15 minutes or until setting point is reached. Skim. Allow to stand 10 minutes before stirring gently and pouring into jars. Seal.

NOTE: *Pressure Cooker (Canner) Lime Marmalade can be made the same way, by substituting limes for oranges and leaving out the lemons.*

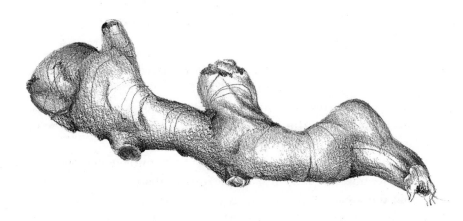

## Pressure Cooker (Canner) Ginger Marmalade

4 Seville (bitter) oranges

1 lemon

5 cm (2 inch) piece
    fresh ginger (ginger
    root), peeled and
    crushed (minced)

3½ cups (28 fl oz)
    water

6 cups (3 lb) sugar

100 g (4 oz) preserved
    ginger

Thinly peel the fruit, then cut the rind in thin slivers and put it into a pressure cooker. Squeeze the juice from the fruit, and add it to the pressure cooker. Tie the pith, seeds and fresh ginger in a muslin (cheesecloth) bag and add it to the pressure cooker with the water. Cover and pressure cook for 20 minutes.

When the pressure drops, remove the cover and extract the muslin bag, squeezing any liquid back into the cooker. Add the sugar and bring slowly to the boil, stirring to dissolve. Finely chop (mince) the preserved ginger and add that too.

Boil rapidly, without stirring, until setting point is reached. Skim. Allow to stand for 10 minutes before stirring gently and pouring into jars. Seal.

*Makes about 10 cups (5 lb)*

———— ◆ ————

*Ginger is probably a native of South-east Asia. It has been used in China and India since ancient times and by the 1st century AD had arrived in the Mediterranean. By the 11th century ginger was well known in England.*

## Brandy Marmalade

1 kg (2 lb) Seville       Juice of 2 lemons
  (bitter) oranges       8 cups (4 lb) sugar
2½ litres (100 fl oz)       ¾ cup (6 fl oz) brandy
  water

Thinly peel the oranges and cut the rind into thin strips, then squeeze out the juice and remove the seeds. Tie the pith and the seeds in a muslin (cheesecloth) bag. Put the peel into a preserving pan with the water, orange and lemon juice, and the muslin bag. Simmer for 1½ hours or until the mixture has reduced to approximately half the original amount. Remove the muslin bag, squeezing the juice into the pan. Add the sugar, stirring until dissolved, then add the brandy and boil rapidly for 20 minutes or until setting point is reached. Allow to stand for 5 minutes. Stir gently, then pour into jars and seal.

*Makes about 14 cups (7 lb)*

## Whisky Marmalade

1½ kg (3 lb) oranges       Juice of 2 lemons
15 cups (120 fl oz)       12 cups (6 lb) sugar
  water       60 ml (2 fl oz) whisky

Wash the oranges in hot water, then remove the peel as thinly as possible and cut into shreds—thin or thick as desired—and put into a preserving pan. Squeeze the oranges and strain the juice into the preserving pan. Tie the seeds, pith and pulp in a muslin (cheesecloth) bag and add to the preserving pan with the water and lemon juice.

Bring to the boil and simmer until the orange peel is tender—about 2 hours. Remove the muslin bag, squeezing any juice back into the pan. Add the sugar and whisky, stirring until the sugar has dissolved. Boil rapidly until setting point is reached. Skim. Allow to stand for 10 minutes before stirring gently and pouring into jars. Seal.

*Makes about 16 cups (8 lb)*

## Pear Marmalade

This is one of the rare marmalades made without citrus fruit. Like citrus marmalade, the fruit is suspended in a soft jelly.

> *1½ kg (3 lb) pears*        *4 cups (2 lb) sugar*
> *Water*

Peel, core and quarter the pears, saving the peel and cores. Put the pears into a preserving pan with the cores and peel tied in a muslin (cheesecloth) bag. Add barely enough water to cover and simmer until tender but not broken. Remove the pears (but not cores and peel) with a slotted spoon and set aside.

Continue boiling the liquid until reduced by half, then remove the cores and peel. Add the sugar, stirring to dissolve, then boil rapidly until setting point is reached. Return pears to the liquid, and when the syrup returns to the boil, remove from the heat. Allow to stand for 5 minutes before stirring gently and pouring into jars. Seal.

*Makes about 7 cups (3½ lb)*

## Quince Marmalade

Quince paste (see page 53) was the original marmalade.

> *Quinces*        *Sugar*
> *Water*

Put the quinces into a preserving pan with enough boiling water to cover and parboil so that the skin will peel off easily. Peel, core and dice the quinces, then weigh them.

Return the diced quinces to the preserving pan with the water used to parboil. There should be barely enough water to cover, so if necessary, remove some of the water. Bring to the boil and simmer for 20 minutes then, for every 1 kg (2 lb) of raw quince, add 1½ cups (12 oz) sugar.

Simmer for 1 hour, stirring occasionally. When it starts to turn a lovely shade of red, begin mashing with a potato masher—there should be no big lumps. Pour into jars and seal when cool.

## Pineapple and Grapefruit Marmalade

In many early marmalade recipes, fruit was soaked for up to 3 days. This preserve requires patience, but this is the way our grandmothers did it. If you want to make a quicker version, skip the first night's soaking.

| | |
|---|---|
| *1 pineapple* | *Water* |
| *1 grapefruit* | *Sugar* |
| *1 lemon* | |

Shred the pineapple—this can be done in a food processor or with a grater. Thinly slice the grapefruit and lemon, then cut the slices into quarters. Remove the seeds and tie in a muslin (cheesecloth) bag. Measure the combined fruit in a measuring jug, then put into a bowl with three times the amount of water and the muslin bag. Leave to stand overnight.

Put the fruit and water into a preserving pan, bring to the boil, then simmer until the rind is tender—this may take 2 hours. Again, leave to stand overnight.

Remove the muslin bag. Measure the fruit and juice, and add an equal measure of sugar. Bring to the boil, stirring to dissolve the sugar. Boil rapidly until setting point is reached—about 1 hour. Leave for 10 minutes then stir before pouring into jars. Seal.

*Makes about 7 cups (3½ lb)*

———— ◆ ————

*The earliest written references to the pineapple come from Columbus and Sir Walter Raleigh who found pineapple growing in the West Indies where it was used for food and wine-making. Today, women in Sri Lanka use raw pineapple rubbed on their skin as a beauty aid.*

### Rhubarb Marmalade

*1 kg (2 lb) rhubarb,*
*trimmed and cut into*
*5 cm (2 inch) pieces*
*3 lemons*

*3 oranges*
*4 cups (2 lb) sugar*
*1½ cups (12 fl oz)*
*water*

Put the rhubarb into a preserving pan. Thinly peel the rind and squeeze juice from the lemons and oranges, and add to the pan. Bring slowly to the boil and simmer for 20 minutes. Add the sugar, stirring to dissolve. Boil rapidly until setting point is reached. Skim. Allow to stand for 5 minutes before stirring gently and pouring into jars. Seal.

*Makes about 7 cups (3½ lb)*

# $\mathscr{F}$RUIT BUTTERS AND CURDS

ruit butters and curds are a delicious alternative to jams, jellies and marmalades. They do not keep as well—once opened they must be stored in the refrigerator—but their lovely flavour ensures that they won't stay on the shelf for long! Unlike jams, jellies and marmalades, no setting test is required, so making butters and curds is a good way for beginners to start home preserving.

*Fruit butters:* These consist of fruit pulp cooked with sugar until all the liquid has evaporated. They are a good way of using the pulp left over from jelly making. Fruit cheeses and pastes are similar but cooking is continued until the mixture is so dry it sets into a shape that you can cut into slices. Serve with cheese or as a sweetmeat.

*Fruit curds:* These are usually made with citrus fruits thickened with sugar, butter and eggs to give a custard-like consistency.

### Fruit Butter

No need to waste the pulp left over from making jelly. Here's a basic recipe for making fruit butter: Pass the pulp through a sieve. Measure the puree, and for each cup (8 oz) of puree, allow ¾ cup (6 oz) sugar. Mix the pulp and sugar together in a preserving pan and if desired, add a stick of cinnamon, a few cloves (in the case of apple) and a strip of lemon peel. Stir over a low heat to dissolve the sugar and cook slowly, stirring frequently, until the puree is thick and translucent. Test by dropping a spoonful onto a plate—if it doesn't ooze water, then it is ready. Remove spices before pouring into bottles and sealing.

## Apple Butter

| | |
|---|---|
| 1 kg (2 lb) cooking apples | 8 cloves |
| 1 teaspoon citric acid | 1 cinnamon stick |
| 1½ cups (12 fl oz) water | 1½ cups (12 oz) sugar |

Chop the apples without peeling or coring. Dissolve the citric acid in the water in a preserving pan. Add the apples, cloves and cinnamon tied in a muslin (cheesecloth) bag, then cook until the apples are pulpy, then push through a sieve. Return the apple puree to the preserving pan, add the sugar, stirring to dissolve, then bring to the boil. Simmer, stirring frequently, until the mixture is thick and translucent. Pour into jars and seal.

*Makes about 4 cups (2 lb)*

## Crock Pot Apple Butter

Slow cooking in a crock pot (slow cooker) is the ideal way to make apple butter—this method also works well with other fruit, such as apricots.

| | |
|---|---|
| Apples | Ground cinnamon |
| Sugar | or ground cloves |

Core and slice the apples—do not peel. Cook the apples without water, in a large covered saucepan over very low heat, until they are soft. Push through a sieve, then measure the puree. Put into a crock pot (slow cooker) and add sugar to equal slightly more than half the amount of apple puree. Add cinnamon or cloves to taste. Cook uncovered on high for 5 hours. Pour into jars.

## Apricot Butter

| | |
|---|---|
| 1 kg (2lb) apricots | Water |
| Juice of ½ lemon | Sugar |

Chop the apricots, remove the stones (pits) and put into a preserving pan with the lemon juice and barely enough water to cover. Bring to the boil and simmer, covered, until the fruit is pulpy. Push the pulp through a sieve or puree in a food processor, then weigh it. Return the puree to the pan and simmer until it starts to thicken. Add sugar equal to half the amount of the weighed puree, and stir until dissolved. Simmer on a low heat, stirring occasionally, until the mixture is thick and there is no excess liquid. Pour into jars and seal.

*Makes about 4 cups (2 lb)*

## Date Paste

A variation on a traditional Jewish recipe—try it as a filling for little pastries to serve with coffee.

| | |
|---|---|
| 225 g (½ lb) dates, pitted | 100 g (4 oz) prunes, pitted |
| 100 g (4 oz) sultanas (golden raisins) | 1 cup (½ lb) sugar |
| 100 g (4 oz) dried apples | 1 cup (8 fl oz) port wine |

Chop the fruit and soak overnight in a bowl with just enough water to cover. Put the fruit and the soaking water into a preserving pan with the sugar and bring to the boil. Simmer gently, stirring constantly, for about 10 minutes. Transfer the hot fruit to a food processor with the port wine and process to a thick, smooth paste. Scrape into jars and seal.

*Makes about 4 cups (2 lb)*

## Gooseberry Curd

1 kg (2 lb)
  gooseberries
2½ cups (20 fl oz)
  water

2 cups (1 lb) sugar
100 g (4 oz) butter,
  unsalted
3 eggs, beaten

Put the gooseberries (no need to top and tail) into a preserving pan
with the water. Bring to the boil and simmer until soft and pulpy. Sieve
the gooseberries and put into the top of a double saucepan (boiler) or
a heat-proof bowl over simmering water. Add the sugar and butter and
stir until the sugar dissolves. Add the eggs and continue cooking, stirring
or whisking frequently, for 30 minutes or until it thickens. Pour into
jars and seal when cool. Store in the refrigerator.

*Makes about 6 cups (3 lb)*

## Lemon Curd

This is the traditional filling for Lemon Meringue Pie.

*Grated rind and*
*juice of 4 lemons*
*2 cups (1 lb) sugar*

*225 g (½ lb) butter*
*6 eggs, beaten*

Put the rind and lemon juice, sugar and butter into the top of a double saucepan (boiler) or a heat-proof bowl over simmering water. Stir until the sugar dissolves, then add the eggs and continue cooking until it thickens, stirring or whisking frequently—about 30 minutes. Pour into jars and seal when cool. Store in the refrigerator.

*Makes about 4 cups (2 lb)*

## Lime Curd

Try Lime Curd in a meringue pie for a delicious variation on that traditional favourite, Lemon Meringue Pie.

*225 g (½ lb) butter,*
*cut into small pieces*
*3 cups (1½ lb) caster*
*(superfine) sugar*

*Grated rind and*
*juice of 10 limes*
*8 eggs, beaten*

Put all ingredients into the top of a double saucepan (boiler) or in a heat-proof bowl placed over simmering water. Heat gently, stirring or whisking frequently, until the mixture thickens—about 30–40 minutes. Pour into jars and seal when cool. Store in the refrigerator.

*Makes about 5 cups (2½ lb)*

## Marrow (Summer Squash) Lemon Curd

*1 marrow (summer*
*squash)*
*For every 200 g (½ lb)*
*marrow (summer*
*squash) puree:*

*1 cup (½ lb) sugar*
*100 g (4 oz) butter*
*Rind and Juice of 3*
*lemons*
*2 eggs*

Peel the marrow, remove the seeds and cut it roughly into cubes. Put into a saucepan with just enough water to prevent sticking, and simmer slowly until soft. Mash, or puree in a food processor. Measure the puree, then calculate the other ingredients in the proportions given above.

Put all ingredients, except the eggs, in the top of a double saucepan (boiler). Heat gently, stirring until the sugar dissolves and the butter melts. Remove from the heat. Beat the eggs and add to the mixture, stirring constantly. Return to the heat and continue stirring until the mixture thickens like a custard. Pour into jars and seal when cool. Store in the refrigerator.

## Orange Curd

*225 g (½ lb) butter,*
*cut into small pieces*
*3 cups (1½ lb) caster*
*(superfine) sugar*

*Grated rind and*
*juice of 6 oranges*
*8 eggs, beaten*

Put all ingredients in the top of a double saucepan (boiler) or in a heat-proof bowl placed over simmering water. Heat gently, stirring or whisking frequently, until the mixture thickens—about 30-40 minutes. Pour into jars and seal when cool. Store in the refrigerator.

*Makes about 6 cups (3 lb)*

## Quince Honey

Fruit honeys are similar to fruit butters, but not quite as thick.

*6 large quinces,*  *2½ cups (20 fl oz) water*
*peeled and cored*  *8 cups (4 lb) sugar*

Finely chop (mince) the quinces in a food processor or mincing machine (food mill), taking care to save all the juice. Bring the water and sugar to the boil, stirring to dissolve the sugar. Add the quince pulp, then boil rapidly for 20 minutes. Pour into jars and seal.

*Makes about 10 cups (5 lb)*

NOTE: *You can substitute 1 small pineapple, shredded, for two of the quinces.*

## Quince Paste

This rich red, jelly-like paste is considered a great delicacy in Spain. It can be cut into squares, rolled in sugar and served as a sweetmeat with coffee, but I like it with a cheese platter. Its sweet, concentrated taste makes a lovely contrast to the sharpness of vintage cheddar.

*Quinces*  *Sugar*

Wash the quinces, rubbing well to remove the down. Put the whole quinces on to the shelves in a moderate oven, preheated to 180°C (350°F) and cook for 2½ hours or until tender. Allow the quinces to cool, then slice, discarding cores and any hard pieces, but not the skin. Rub through a sieve, then weigh the puree and add an equal amount of sugar.

Put the mixture into a preserving pan, and bring to the boil, stirring constantly. Continue to cook on a low heat, stirring constantly, until the paste thickens and begins to come away from the bottom of the pan. Be careful because the boiling paste will spit. Remove from the heat and continue stirring until it stops bubbling. Pour the paste into a shallow, rectangular swiss roll (jelly roll) pan and leave overnight.

Next day, put the pan of paste into the oven switched to its lowest temperature. Leave until the paste dries out and is quite firm—it will take several hours. It should be a rich, translucent red. Cut into serving pieces and wrap in plastic (cling) wrap or aluminium foil. Store in airtight containers or in the refrigerator.

# FRUIT LIQUEURS

M aking fruit liqueurs may not be the most economical form of
preserving, but it's fun!

### Apple Brandy

| 2½ cups (20 fl oz) apple juice | 2 cups (1 lb) sugar |
| | 4 cups (32 fl oz) brandy |

Put the apple juice and sugar into a large saucepan and bring to the
boil, stirring to dissolve. Simmer until the syrup reduces to about 1 cup
(8 fl oz), skim and leave to cool. Mix with the brandy and pour into
bottles. Seal. Leave for at least 1 month before using.

*Makes about 5 cups (40 fl oz)*

### Apricot Liqueur

| 500 g (1 lb) apricots, halved and stoned (pitted) | 1 cup (8 fl oz) water |
| | 3 cups (24 fl oz) white wine |
| 2 cups (1 lb) sugar | 2 cups (16 fl oz) gin |

Put the apricots, sugar and water into a saucepan and bring slowly to the boil, stirring to dissolve the sugar. Simmer, covered, for 5 minutes, then add the wine and heat. When almost at boiling point, remove from the heat and cool. Transfer to a large jar and add the gin. Stir well, then seal and store in a cool, dark place for 5 days. Strain through muslin (cheesecloth) into a jug and pour into bottles. Seal. Leave for at least 1 month before using.

*Makes about 6 cups (48 fl oz)*

## Blackberry (Bramble) Liqueur

| | |
|---|---|
| 500 g (1 lb) black-<br>berries (brambles)<br>(frozen are fine) | 2 cups (1 lb) sugar<br>1 cup (8 fl oz) water<br>3 cups (32 fl oz) gin |

Put the blackberries, sugar and water into a saucepan and bring slowly to the boil, stirring to dissolve the sugar. Simmer for about 20 minutes, or until the liquid is thick and syrupy. Strain through muslin (cheesecloth) into a jug and add the gin. Stir and pour into bottles. Seal. Leave for at least 1 month before using.

*Makes about 5 cups (40 fl oz)*

NOTE: *You can substitute raspberries, either fresh or frozen, for blackberries.*

## Cherry Brandy

| | |
|---|---|
| 500 g (1 lb) cherries,<br>pitted | 2 cups (1 lb) sugar<br>4 cups (32 fl oz) brandy |

Put the cherries and sugar into a large jar, seal and keep in the refrigerator for 2 days, shaking the jar occasionally. Add the brandy to the jar, and leave for 3 months in a cool dark place, shaking the jar occasionally. Strain through muslin (cheesecloth) into a jug and pour liquid into bottles. Seal.

*Makes about 5 cups (40 fl oz)*

## Brandied Cherries

| | |
|---|---|
| 6 cups (3 lb) sugar<br>4 cups (32 fl oz)<br>water | 1 kg (2 lb) cherries,<br>pitted<br>3 cups (24 fl oz) brandy |

Put the sugar and water into a saucepan and bring to the boil, stirring to dissolve the sugar. Simmer for 5 minutes. Add the cherries and cook for about 1 minute. Using a slotted spoon, transfer the cherries to jars.

Skim the syrup if necessary, then continue boiling without stirring until a teaspoon dropped in cold water forms a soft ball when rolled between your fingers. Add the brandy and stir to combine before pouring over the cherries. Make sure that the cherries are completely covered. Seal. Leave for 3 months before using.

*Makes about 14 cups (7 lb)*

## Cumquat (Kumquat) Brandy

500 g (1 lb) cumquats (kumquats)　　1 cup (8 fl oz) water
2 cups (1 lb) sugar　　3 cups (24 fl oz) brandy

Prick the cumquats with a darning needle and put into a large jar. Bring the sugar and water slowly to the boil, stirring to dissolve the sugar. Simmer for 5 minutes. Cool. Combine the syrup and brandy and pour it over the cumquats. Seal. Leave for 2 months in a cool, dark place. Strain off the cumquats (these may be eaten with ice-cream and a little of the liqueur) and pour the liquid into a bottle. Or leave the cumquats and liqueur in the jar and use as required.

*Makes about 6 cups (3 lb) with cumquats*

## Currant Liqueur

500 g (1 lb) black or redcurrants　　½ cup (4 oz) sugar
2 cups (16 fl oz) gin

Put the currants into a bowl and add the sugar. Using a potato masher, mash the currants and sugar together, then add the gin. Stir thoroughly, then pour into a jar and seal. Leave for 6 weeks. Strain through muslin (cheesecloth) into a jug, then squeeze the muslin over the jug to extract any juice. Pour the liquid into bottles and seal. Leave for at least 1 week before using.

*Makes about 3 cups (24 fl oz)*

## Brandied Grapes

Grapes are left in bunches for a spectacular effect. Great on a cheese platter, and you can pour the syrup into small glasses to serve with it.

| | |
|---|---|
| *500 g (1 lb) black*<br>  *(red) grapes in*<br>  *bunches* | *2 cups (1 lb) sugar*<br>*Brandy* |

Prick each grape in a few places with a needle. Put bunches of grapes into a wide-mouthed jar, and sprinkle with sugar. Pour in enough brandy to cover the fruit completely, then seal. Gently shake the jar a couple of times a day until the sugar dissolves—about 2 weeks. Grapes are then ready to eat, but will be better if left for a month.

*Makes about 4 cups (2 lb)*


## Lime Shrub

Shrub is a mixed drink of rum, fruit juice and sugar. In this recipe lime provides a delicious tart flavour.

| | |
|---|---|
| *1 lime*<br>*2 cups (1 lb) sugar*<br>*1 cup (8 fl oz) lime*<br>  *juice* | *3 cups (24 fl oz)*<br>  *white (light) rum* |

Slice the lime and put into a large jar. Bring the sugar and lime juice slowly to the boil, stirring to dissolve the sugar. Simmer for 5 minutes. Skim and cool. Combine the syrup with the rum and pour over the sliced lime. Seal. Leave for 1 month in a cool, dark place. Strain into a jug and pour the liquid into a bottle.

*Makes about 4 cups (32 fl oz)*

## Orange Vodka

Flavoured vodkas are popular in Russia where they drink vodka straight—
we tend to add flavourings when we drink it.

*2½ cups (20 fl oz)
orange juice,
strained*

*4 cups (2 lb) sugar
4½ cups (36 fl oz)
vodka*

Put the orange juice and sugar into a large saucepan and bring slowly
to the boil, stirring to dissolve the sugar. Simmer for 10 minutes, skim
and cool. Add the vodka and pour it into a jar. Seal. Leave for 2 weeks
in a cool, dark place, shaking the jar every day, then leave for another
4 weeks undisturbed. Strain the liquid through muslin (cheesecloth) into
a jug, then pour into bottles and seal.

*Makes about 8 cups (64 fl oz)*

## Brandied Peaches

*1 kg (2 lb) peaches
6 cups (3 lb) sugar*

*4 cups (32 fl oz) water
3 cups (24 fl oz) brandy*

Plunge the peaches into boiling water for about 1 minute, then remove
the skins. Halve the peaches and remove the stones (pits). Bring the
sugar and water to the boil, stirring to dissolve the sugar, then simmer
for 5 minutes. Add the peaches and cook for 3 minutes, then remove
from the heat. Using a slotted spoon, transfer the peaches to jars.

Bring the syrup to the boil and simmer, without stirring, until a
teaspoon dropped in cold water forms a soft ball when rolled between
your fingers. Add the brandy and stir to combine before pouring over
the peaches, making sure that the peaches are completely covered. Seal.
Leave for 3 months before using.

**Brandied Apricots**: Substitute apricots for peaches but do not remove
skins.

*Makes about 8 cups (4 lb)*

## Peach Liqueur

| | |
|---|---|
| *6 peaches, pitted* | *4 cups (32 fl oz)* |
| *3 cups (1½ lb) sugar* | *brandy* |

Chop the peaches and put into a jar with the sugar. Keep in the refrigerator overnight, then add the brandy. Seal and return to the fridge for 1 week. Strain through muslin (cheesecloth) into a jug and pour into bottles. Seal.

*Makes about 5 cups (40 fl oz)*

## Brandied Pears

| | |
|---|---|
| 3 cups (1½ lb) sugar | 1 kg (2 lb) pears, peeled, |
| 2 cups (16 fl oz) | but left whole |
| water | 2 cups (16 fl oz) brandy |

Put the sugar and water into a saucepan and bring to the boil, stirring to dissolve the sugar. Simmer for 5 minutes. Add the pears and cook for about 10 minutes or until tender. Using a slotted spoon, transfer the pears to wide-necked jars. Continue boiling the syrup for 5 minutes. Add the brandy and stir to combine before pouring over the pears, making sure the pears are completely covered. Seal. Leave for 1 month before using.

*Makes about 7 cups (3½ lb)*

## Pear Brandy

| | |
|---|---|
| 2½ cups (20 fl oz) | 2 cups (1 lb) sugar |
| pear juice, strained | 4 cups (32 fl oz) |
| (canned is fine) | brandy |

Put the pear juice and sugar into a large saucepan and bring to the boil, stirring to dissolve. Simmer until the syrup reduces to about 1 cup (8 fl oz), skim and leave to cool. Mix with the brandy and pour into bottles. Seal. Leave for at least 1 month before using.

**Pear Vodka:** You can make an excellent Pear Vodka by substituting vodka for brandy.

*Makes about 5 cups (40 fl oz)*

———— ◆ ————

*There are over 5000 varieties of pear in existence worldwide.*

## Pineapple Liqueur

1 fresh pineapple,       ½ cup (4 oz) sugar
    peeled, cored and      4½ cups (36 fl oz) gin
    chopped

Crush (mince) the pineapple with the sugar in a food processor, and pour into a large jar. Add the gin and stir. Seal, and leave for 2 months in a cool, dark place. Strain the liqueur through muslin (cheesecloth) into a jug, then pour into bottles. Keep for at least another week before using—the longer the better.

*Makes about 6 cups (48 fl oz)*

## Pineapple Shrub

3 cups (24 fl oz)      4 cups (2 lb) sugar
    pineapple juice,      4½ cups (36 fl oz)
    strained (canned      white (light) rum
    is fine)

Put the pineapple juice and sugar into a large saucepan and bring slowly to the boil, stirring to dissolve the sugar. Simmer for 10 minutes, then skim and cool. Add the rum and pour into a jar. Seal. Leave for 2 weeks in a cool dark place, shaking the jar every day, then leave for another 4 weeks undisturbed. Strain the liquid through muslin (cheesecloth) into a jug, then pour into bottles and seal.

*Makes about 8 cups (64 fl oz)*

————— ◆ —————

*Instant coffee evolved in the 1930s when
coffee producers wanted a method
of preserving coffee as the flavour of the
ground bean deteriorates so quickly.*

## Strawberry Liqueur

500 g (1 lb) straw-
berries
1 cup (½ lb) caster
(superfine) sugar

½ cup (4 fl oz) water
2 cups (16 fl oz)
brandy

Chop the strawberries and put into a jar. Put the sugar and water into a saucepan and bring slowly to the boil, stirring to dissolve. Simmer for 5 minutes, then cool and stir into strawberries. Add the brandy, seal and keep in the fridge for 2 days, shaking the jar occasionally. Strain through muslin (cheesecloth) into a jug, then pour into a bottle and seal. Leave for at least 1 month before using.

*Makes about 4 cups (32 fl oz)*

## Coffee Liqueur

This isn't a fruit liqueur, but I've included it because it is popular, easy to make and, like fruit liqueurs, ideal for drinking with after-dinner coffee.

1 cup (½ lb) soft
brown sugar
½ cup (4 fl oz) water

6 teaspoons instant
coffee
3 cups (24 fl oz) brandy

Put the sugar and water into a saucepan and bring slowly to the boil, stirring to dissolve the sugar. Simmer for a few minutes. Add the coffee, stir and cool. Pour into a jar and stir in the brandy. Seal and leave in a cool, dark place for 2 weeks. Strain through muslin (cheesecloth) into a jug and pour into bottles. Seal.

*Makes about 4 cups (32 fl oz)*

# $\mathcal{I}$NDEX